DANCING
IN THE
WIND

DANCING
IN THE
WIND

SANDRA WEATHERWAX

TATE PUBLISHING
AND **ENTERPRISES, LLC**

Published by Tate Publishing & Enterprises, LLC
127 E. Trade Center Terrace | Mustang, Oklahoma 73064 USA
1.888.361.9473 | www.tatepublishing.com

Tate Publishing is committed to excellence in the publishing industry. The company reflects the philosophy established by the founders, based on Psalm 68:11,
"The Lord gave the word and great was the company of those who published it."

Book design copyright © 2014 by Tate Publishing, LLC. All rights reserved.
Cover design by Gian Philipp Rufin
Interior design by Jomel Pepito

Published in the United States of America

ISBN: 978-1-63063-901-3
1. Medical / Veterinary Medicine / Equine
2. Science / Life Sciences / Zoology / Mammals
14.04.25

For all of my family,
Those who are here on earth
And those who have already had their moving day.

ACKNOWLEDGMENTS

I thank the Lord Jesus Christ for giving me the words to write.

A deep and grateful thanks to all my encouragers. Rick Barry, an author and editor who was there in the beginning. Ellen Augustine, a language arts teacher who understood my writing and pushed me not to give up. Tanya Paulus, James and Marilyn Keene, and Monica Lasater, friends who gave me so much encouragement and love when I needed it. My sister-in-law Barb Vanderbor who listened, read my work, and continually asked, "How is the writing going?" Love you, Barb, and thank you.

Special thanks to Tracey LaPierre for her dedication and wonderful help with the final manuscript submission.

Thanks also to family members, Heidi Linder, Christina Ashbaugh, and Hal Knight who helped me down the finish line to production.

A big thanks to the publishers who gave me the opportunity to see my story in print.

PREFACE

This true story is not about celebrities, just a family living the life they have been given, making mistakes, but learning and traveling upward. My desire is for the reader to understand how the love of God and his promises are greater than any earthly tragedy.

When harsh winds blow and you are not hanging on to God, he is hanging on to you. My heart and soul have been lifted through the years by the wonder and courage of the many beautiful students coming to LoveWay's therapeutic horseback riding school. They are glorious examples of the true and simple joys of life. Walking up the hill to the LoveWay fields and arena, you *know* God is there. To participate in the miracles of challenged riders and faithful steeds, you *know* God is there.

Animals were always part of our life, true gifts from God. Our Florida cougar BSOB was certainly a gift for my paraplegic husband, Gary. I want all to understand even though we loved BSOB dearly, I do not wish for animals to be taken from the wild and have a life in captivity. He was a little cat, with a future of a pen for life. There are many exotic animals living in captivity in terrible conditions. People do not realize all that is involved in the care of a wild animal. May God help us to preserve the habitat for his wild creatures. We need to look at our planet and our lives as an exciting and wonderful gift, then press on to open our eyes and ears to absorb it's beauty—then radiate God's love to *all*.

CONTENTS

CHAPTER 1

Smooth voices of the world
beckon with subtle songs.
Melodies wrap around my heart
and bind me to their wrongs.
Pillars great before me rise,
applaud my every whim.
I smile and revel in my strength
but never see the sin.
Winds change, the music stops,
quiet screams too loud.
My frantic soul is reaching out
to find the hand of God.

The smell and sounds of the stable were a sweet comfort as horses gently snickered at my clumsy banging in the early morning light. Yearning to be drawn into this peaceful escape from creeping troubles, I busied myself with the chores at hand. Indiana spring was upon us, and the horses were anxious to be out.

Softly puffing a gentle breath on the outstretched nose of Hooligan, our Arabian stallion, I laughed and hugged him close. With my arms circled around his long neck, I felt his total acceptance of me. Hooligan laid his head on my shoulder and waited patiently for my next move…sweet feed in his manger.

If only my marriage could be basted with more acceptance. Lately, accusations were the general climate of our home, and there wasn't a secure footing for even a discussion of our problems. Running down separate paths, we collided once in a while, and it was not always a happy occasion. However, one thing we shared was confusion about life, a feeling of discontent and searching.

Some days were taut as a bowstring ready to fire. Both of us weary of the so-called rat race and having sold our manufacturing business we had even considered moving to the deep Canadian woods! There was complete disillusionment and a building aversion to our compromising of all that we knew was wrong in our lifestyle.

Grimacing as I cleaned the horse's hoof, I reflected on the many hours that our fifteen-year-old daughter, Laurie, and I already spent alone in our castle on the hill. Visualizing an even more isolated woodland life in Canada did not require great imagination, and I would bet my bottom dollar that Gary, my husband, would have a plane that *he* would be flying in and out.

Smiling at the joyful and contented crunching as every delicate nose dug into the feed, I flipped a bucket upside down and sat down to enjoy the pleasant scene. Now the morning sun was high enough to sneak in the windows, bouncing light off tails that would soon be flying in play when let out to pasture.

After the last bit of grain had been scrounged from the feed boxes and the horses were racing in their fields, I began to muck out the stalls. The old wheelbarrow emitted a friendly creak when filled, so I hummed along as I pushed it. There was special pleasure in filling each clean stall with soft, creamy colored wood shavings.

Through the open door, the wind shifted and whipped up a miniature whirlwind of shavings on the stable floor. It also blew in the familiar hulk of Ali Baa-Baa, our pet ram. Not a humble animal, he always arrived with a bit too much arrogance.

I had to grin, thinking of a week earlier when Ali Baa-Baa had caused a real ruckus. *Someone* had been leaving the water faucet near the back door of our house turned on. Gary, deep red in the face and with his temper nearing the bursting point, sat Laurie and me down at the kitchen table.

"That water has run so much, there is now a frog-filled stream in the backyard. It is going to stop!" he said, his voice thundering.

In the middle of his loud lecture, we all heard the familiar squeak of the outside faucet. The three of us jumped up, raced to the back door, trying to squeeze through at the same time. Peering around the corner of the house, we observed a nonchalant Ali Baa-Baa turn the faucet handle with his mouth, get his drink, and casually stroll away. It must be, we decided, too long a walk down to the pond for overweight ram.

As I sat on my bucket and recalled our laughter, I gave Ali a hug, then spotted his wet feet. Gary wired the faucet shut after we discovered the culprit, but evidently, that hadn't solved the problem.

"Well, you've loosened the wire and done it again, you crazy animal! Let's go fix it," I grumbled.

Replacing the old pitchfork and shovel on their hooks on the barn wall, I turned to admire my work, then stood for a moment, just staring. Sighing, I thought to myself, we could lose all this! The large corporation that bought our business had systematically begun to break every agreement, including our payoff and Gary's workout time with them.

"I can't believe it," Gary had steamed a few days before. "They cheapened everything, especially where it doesn't show! They have no feeling for the dealers, employees, and for that matter, *us!*"

I turned to leave the barn. Kismet and Prince, our shepherd and collie dogs that had been sleeping by the door, arose obediently to follow Ali and me up the hill. Heading for the water faucet, I had to step carefully to avoid tripping over animals as we trudged along.

Our beautiful, but pretentious house stood atop a hill, silhouetted against the sky like a fort or, as one friend jokingly chided, a holiday inn. Before the animals and I reached the house, I heard the phone ringing, so I broke into a run. I flung open the door, and the animal parade followed inside. Ali Baa-Baa shoved his way past us all and then headed for the newly purchased bag of Purina Dog Chow.

Out of breath, I snatched up the receiver. A sharp, controlled voice spilled out the words, "Mrs. Weatherwax? We have been trying to reach you all morning! There has been an accident. Your husband is in the hospital and is not expected to live. You must hurry!"

The phone seemed to turn cold in my hand. I could not speak; my voice was lost. Finally, I managed to whisper, "I'm coming," and I stood in shock before slowly placing the phone receiver back in the cradle.

As I yanked off my boots and put on shoes, my mind was a whirlwind of confusion. Gary in an accident? What could have happened? He left early that morning to help a friend with his production line in a small nearby town. I shooed the animals outside and dashed from the house in a blur. The hospital was twenty minutes away. I don't remember the drive, but I can still feel the nausea that engulfed me on entering the emergency room. Low moans and crying came from a side room.

Confused and feeling a suffocating dread, I managed the words, "I'm Mrs. Weatherwax."

A nurse touched my arm and led me to a seat. "The doctor will be here in a moment," she said soothingly.

"Who is crying in the other room?" I blurted out.

"The driver of the other car has died," she replied.

Suspended in this nightmare, I waited for the blow. As though paralyzed, I sat immobile, staring at the bits of sawdust that still clung to my hands.

A brush of movement brought my eyes up to lock on those of the doctor before me. "Your husband is alive, but his back is broken. I don't know the complete extent of the damage. We will operate when his blood pressure is stabilized. At the moment, he is paralyzed from the neck down." He then gently informed me I could see Gary.

Walking in the room, I was astonished to see him awake and coherent. Relief poured through me as we talked and reassured each other that everything was going to be all right. My heart's old love for him flamed, and then tears began to flow as I left to sign the medical papers and call my mother.

Mother lived nearby and came immediately.

"I must call Jo," Mother said calmly. My sister Josephine lived just blocks away from the hospital. She joined us within minutes.

"Sandy, if there is anything I can do, fly him anywhere or bring in another doctor—anything, just tell me!" cried Jo.

The local doctor appeared and said with urgency, "I don't feel Gary can handle being moved. He is in shock, and his blood pressure jumps up and down like a yo-yo. There's an excellent surgeon within thirty minutes from here. I don't know if Gary will survive the operation, but we must move quickly."

"I don't know what to do," I cried, sobbing to Mother and Jo. "I want him to have the best surgeon possible, but I have to consider the doctor's advice."

"Please, Mrs. Weatherwax, we must move!" the doctor pleaded.

My voice shook as I said, "Call the surgeon here."

Gary's blood pressure finally stabilized, and he was hustled into the operating room. Then began the long wait while the three of us kept vigil and waited for news. During that wait, the police officer found us and brought us answers to some of our questions. "It appears the other driver was traveling at a high rate of speed when he ran a stop sign. The pickup your husband was driving was demolished, and he was thrown out, probably hitting his back on the door. He must have seen the other car coming because skid marks show he tried to stop. It's amazing he was awake and actually able to talk to the ambulance driver and medics when they arrived on the scene. In fact, it's amazing he's alive at all."

My mother, sister, and I sat quietly, saying very little. We didn't know if Gary would make it through the operation, so we decided to wait for the outcome before we went after Laurie, who was still at school. I remembered other close calls Gary had lived through. Would this be different? Somehow, I could not accept the fact that he might die. Gary was tough, real tough, I told myself. He would make it!

Hours later, a weary, subdued doctor came to deliver a mixture of good and bad news. "Gary survived the operation. We wired his back together. Although his spinal cord was almost completely severed, he may regain the use of his arms, but he will never walk again," he reported in an emotionless tone.

My mind focused on the fact that he was alive, and the rest, I shoved aside.

It would be some time before I would be allowed to see Gary. Mother left to pick up Laurie, and I urged my sister to go home to her family. Feeling the need for air, I rode the elevator to the main floor and stepped outside. A slight breeze danced in the trees and rustled the branches. It sang a soothing song, but the breeze also carried the scent of an upcoming storm. Before long, the leaves would be ripped from stems and tossed about.

I wanted to cry, but no tears came. Instead, a hundred jumbled questions and thoughts ran through my mind. How would Gary face what happened? This bright spring day had turned upside down.

Filling my lungs with a deep breath, I stepped back inside the glass doors into the uncharted world. At that moment, I could not foresee or comprehend the new path that our little family would find.

Laurie arrived at the hospital with my mother. The flashing of anger in her brown eyes shot me full of darts as if I were a traitor.

"Why didn't you come for me right away?" she questioned.

I tried to explain the minute-to-minute crisis and struggle for her father's life, but no explanation softened her. In my own heart, I felt she was right. We should have sent someone for her right away.

A pretty, smiling nurse interrupted, "You may go in and see Gary now."

Entering a small room within the intensive care ward, we faced an unconscious figure hooked up to a mass of tubes and not looking like anyone I knew. Laurie's eyes searched mine for answers. My heart was laid bare. I could not cover my fears. We both cried tears cleansing the emotional strain between us. Each hour, we were permitted to go in for a few minutes. As the weight of the day slowly gave into the dark of night, the wind flattened raindrops against the hospital windows.

Time seemed to almost stop. Mother drove Laurie home to care for the animals and then to her home for a sleepless night. I decided to remain at the hospital. Sitting in the waiting room, I felt as if I had been suddenly whisked to another planet, and I tried to digest the events of the day. Even the language was foreign to me, and I struggled to interpret new talk of nerves, catheters, L4 and L5.

As I sat there alone, vivid memories from the 1950s burst into my head and started to play back to me like a projector loaded with my favorite movie. I remembered the first time I saw Gary. We both attended school in a small, nearby town. He was being hauled off to the principal's office by the shirt collar, swinging his fist all the way. Smiling primly, I had thought what an awful little brat that boy must be and I wanted nothing to do with him. Years later, sometime during my freshman year of high school, the negative impression of that nasty little brat changed to interest in his confident, feisty boldness. My young romantic heart found itself opening to his attentions.

I could see him standing before me with his blond hair styled in the latest rage, the DA, of course! His rolled-up T-shirt sleeves held a pack of cigarettes and rust-colored pegged pants revealed bowlegs. The foundation for this figure was a pair of white buck shoes. Gary's deep brown eyes looked unabashedly into mine, and I fell hard. I knew there could never be another. I was sure this man could capture the moon and every star for me. I flung my heart at him to catch and hold next to his. He told me I was his world. I fell harder.

Through high school, we were considered a couple. Gary's jealousy became legend, which was constantly fueled by my immature actions. Too often, I gave no thought to his short temper and the consequences, so we experienced a fiery time during our dating years. Our marriage wasn't dull either, certainly not peaceful. Gary's temper did not improve although his jealousy did and was replaced by a much less attentive husband. When first married I still relied on my old childish tactics to get attention, and the green eyed monster began to raise its ugly head in *my* heart instead. Our relationship had no spiritual foundation, just strong physical attraction and our love for each other sewn together with possessiveness.

A kind face and gentle touch interrupted my emotional reminiscing. "Mrs. Weatherwax, why don't you go home and get some rest?" a nurse urged. "It will be better for Gary if you are strong when he is awake. Go on home. We'll call you if there's any change."

I thanked her and slipped into his room one last time that evening. Staring at the wall of monitors and suddenly feeling exhausted, I took the nurse's advice.

Outside, the rain had stopped. Slick, deserted streets gleamed in the illumination of streetlights, and I felt small and alone. The drive home seemed long and somehow frightening. I hadn't prayed for a long time. Would God still listen? Was this all some kind of punishment? I remembered that as a little girl,

I thought about God a lot. I was awed by the Christ child but afraid of God.

At summer Bible school, I stood with all the other children, and we were asked if we could hear Jesus knocking at our heart's door. I thought all the children in the room could hear my heart pounding. I went forward and asked Jesus to enter my heart, but I never told anyone at home. What had happened to that little girl? Suddenly feeling heavy-laden with my sins, I was sure God wouldn't want to help me. Gary and I had been living and dancing to the world's songs, but now, the notes were hollow with no ring of joy.

"Please, God, help me," I pleaded but didn't believe he would answer.

Finally driving up our long lane, glad to see some lights were on, I plodded up the hill and turned off the outside faucet. Leaping and barking their welcome, the dogs were overjoyed to see me. I let them in to the house and then fell on the floor, hugging them. That's where I awoke a few hours later.

The shrill ring of the telephone jolted me up, and I began a race with time that would engulf me for months. The news was out, and everyone had questions. How did the accident happen? Is Gary going to be all right? Are you all right? What are the injuries? How long will he be in the hospital? Can we visit him soon? I couldn't take two steps away from the phone. The ringing was continuous. Finally, I just ignored it, threw cold water in my face, fed the animals, and ran to the car for the drive back to the hospital.

Life in Gary's little cubicle was the same, but at least, it was life. I called Mother and Laurie with news he was alive. Mother kept Laurie home from school and promised to bring her to see Gary later. Settling once more in the waiting room, I gazed out the window at the soft spring day fresh from yesterday's rain. The hospitals lighting seemed so cold and harsh, I longed to bring some of springtime into Gary's room.

A nurse stopped at the door. "Gary is asking for you," she announced.

I rushed to the intensive care ward and into the small room that confined my husband. Doctors were there talking to him, and his eyes told me he was relieved to see me. He was still confused from heavy medication but trying to be cooperative.

"Do you feel this?" they were saying as they pricked his feet and legs with pins.

Gary shook his head. "No."

"Can you feel this?" one asked as he pricked Gary's arms.

"Yes, a little," was his reply. But he still did not move his arms.

Gary drifted in and out of consciousness all day. At one point, he asked me to push down on his legs. He thought they were floating up from the bed.

When the surgeon arrived, I seized the opportunity to ask, "Will you explain, in a little more detail, the injury Gary has suffered and what to expect?"

He was gruff and short with me, "It's too hard to explain to a layperson!"

I was stunned and turned away with stinging in my eyes and heart. "But this layperson is his wife," I mumbled as I walked away.

Then, in the waiting room, a wall of people met me. Each one told a story about Gary. Some told how good he was to work for; others shared how he had helped them financially. Most of these stories I had never heard. The smile on my face became fixed as I thanked them each for coming, at the same time realizing how far apart Gary and I had grown.

Then began a routine that seemed endless: hurry to the hospital and ache for the sameness of Gary's days. He would become confused and think I had not been there at all when I stepped out for a few minutes. Then came a time when his nerve endings were so sensitive that he could not stand even the weight of the sheet on him. He would sweat and shake at the same time, and the pain was great.

Some days, I walked across the street to the park for a few minutes and slammed tennis balls against a wall, trying to beat out my frustrations.

Dear God, when did I leave you? Did you leave me?

CHAPTER 2

There is always the pain
that tears and rips apart.
Though shaking, weak, and cold,
flames still burn in his heart.
He does not cry or scream.
He does not beg or whine.
But eyes reveal the suffering
when turned to look in mine.
The pain sometimes engulfs
the silence sick and deep.
I pray a small reprieve
to let his body sleep.

Yes, there was pain. Would it ever end or even ease? I knew Gary must have been asking that question with more fervor than I.

The Stryker bed was to become a part of Gary's life for a long time. His spine had to remain unmoved where it was wired together. He was sandwiched in the circle of steel, turned face down, then face up, day and night. He would eat in the facedown position, which he abhorred. The food directly in front of his face was unappetizing and hard to swallow. Most friends came to visit while he was in that position for the evening meal. We laughed about this as Gary felt he got to know people in new and interesting ways while observing them from the waist down.

He chuckled. "I now recognize my friends by their shoes."

Gary was a fighter, and so he fought. He slowly regained the use of his arms, along with glimmers of his old sense of humor. I marveled when previously unseen colors of Gary emerged—patience and acceptance. Weeks slowly ground by, and many friends came to visit, often to retell and savor old stories. There is a certain charm and hilarity in old tales, even those that are surrounded by desperation at the actual time of their birth.

Many of those stories took place in the late fifties when we were first married and money was scarce. Gary never seemed to lack enthusiasm for exciting projects. For example, once he had crafted a huge pontoon boat of old barrels and with a paddle wheel, no less! This creation sported a series of dubious motors that Gary was constantly tinkering on. One summer, he lived just to give friends rides on the river. Growing up by the river and living close to it now, he was still drawn to spend time on its waters. There was one gentleman, however, who always eyed his endeavors with great caution, thinking it over. There was probably more than one.

"Oh, come on," Gary coaxed him. "Meet us at the dock after work, and I'll take you on a relaxing ride. The fall foliage is glorious right now."

A little before the appointed time, Gary and I were getting the boat ready, and he said, "Go with me on a quick warm-up jaunt before my friend arrives."

I accepted and relaxed in an old canvas sling back deck chair. I was wearing a corduroy Rah-rah jacket leftover from school days. The weak autumn sun felt good on my face, and I leaned back with closed eyes to enjoy the warmth.

Gary continued fussing over the motor, and few minutes later, I opened my eyes to see the riverbank coming up fast and at a point where many limbs overhung the water.

"Gary! We're heading for a tree!" I yelled.

Gary's back was turned, and his head was down by the motor, so my words were lost in the roar. I tried to scramble out of the canvas chair but didn't quite make it. A limb slammed into the back of the sling chair with such force that I was catapulted into the air. As my flailing body executed a perfect somersault, the boat chugged out from under me, and I hit the water, where I immediately sank to the bottom.

Clawing my way upward, I tried to keep my lace-less saddle shoes on. The heavy corduroy jacket weighed me down like an anchor. Finally breaking the surface, I was greeted by a helping hand and Gary's contorted face as he struggled desperately not to laugh. But of course, he did not succeed.

He did stop laughing long enough to catch his breath and ask, "Did you see any fish down there?"

We immediately headed for the dock in silence except for the droning and sometimes coughing motor.

By this time, our friend stood on the pier with his wide eyes on me as we maneuvered the craft in. Shivering and with nose in the air, I sloshed off the boat, dripping and glaring. The friend politely declined the scenic autumn ride.

Now, years later, sitting in the hospital room, we laughed about that day, and I touched Gary's clammy skin. *He* was the one shivering now and sweating at the same time. His sensory nerves were damaged, and we would eventually realize this to be a lifelong problem.

Gary gripped my hand. His body shaking so hard, he shook the bed and hung on until the next dose of medication.

Laurie was back in school, and at home, I depended on her to do a lot of chores. We had been close before Gary's accident, but now, I was not seeing her enough. Our relationship became strained, obviously due to the amount of time I spent at the hospital but also due to the addition of a boy in her life.

Laurie always loved her grandma and grandpa Knight. When Grandpa Knight passed away, Laurie was devastated. She had spent many hours with her grandparents, while Gary and I were building our business. They loved and enjoyed her tremendously, but a time would come when Gary and I would regret the many hours we had missed being with her.

Weeks dragged into months. Gary longed to come home, but the doctors would only talk rehabilitation. He must have rehabilitation, or he would not be able to do anything for himself, they all insisted.

"Sandy, I just want to come home," he said. "I don't need any help. I can do it on my own. I know I can. I don't need someone to teach me to dress. I have you to help me do that! I can't stand any more confinement. We can work on rehabilitation at home. It will work, if I just go home!"

The doctors were adamant, and after many arguments, Gary consented. He would be going to a large rehab center hours away. Gary would have to stay there for a while before he would be allowed to come home on weekends. The length of his stay was an unknown.

"I'll put everything I have into it, and I will come home walking," Gary said with his fire and determination.

In an essay Laurie wrote for school, she firmly stated, "I *know* my father will walk again!" I guess we were accustomed to him beating the odds.

We made the trip to the rehab with the help of a friend. We were all tense, not knowing what to expect. We pushed Gary in his wheelchair through the doors of yet another challenge. My shoes clicked and echoed in the long halls as Gary's chair silently rolled into a world populated with wheelchairs. I sensed his apprehension, and so I replayed the doctors' advice in my head.

After checking in, we rode the wide elevator to Gary's floor where he was put in bed. We passed the afternoon with small talk, and soon, it was time to leave. I could barely look at his pleading brown eyes that begged for just a few more minutes.

"Laurie and I will be back this weekend," I promised.

"I know. It just seems like you will so far away," he replied in a soft and shaky voice.

"The time will fly you will be kept so busy." I grinned. "No more soft life for you. They will make you work! And no flirting with that cute girl in the wheelchair we passed on the way up!"

Gary managed a smile, and after a long embrace, we left.

Our friend talked a lot on the way home. I can't remember about what. So much lay heavy on my mind. I was behind on everything around the house—bills, Laurie's affairs and needs—and I could use some sleep. I knew Gary would be expecting visits often. I, in turn, desperately longed for someone to put their arms around me and tell me everything would be all right. At home, I threw myself into housework and chores, trying to untangle one mess after another.

I again sought the peaceful solace of the barn and my mother's home. My eyes were suddenly opened to the deep chasm of loss my mother must have felt with Dad. They had been so close.

At the rehabilitation center, Gary threw himself into therapy; he begged to do double time. A staff member arrived to sign him up for the psychiatrist as part of the new patient routine. Gary was quick to inform him that he was here for the lower end, not upper. Another poor soul asked if Gary would like to make piggy-shaped cutting boards. He replied through clenched teeth, "I made those in grade school. I make other things now. Let's just work on walking!"

Gary was fitted with braces, but he was paralyzed as far up as right below his arms and the braces proved nearly impossible to be of use. Discouragement began to overtake him. Laurie and I visited on weekends, and we noticed he never wanted to eat in the cafeteria with the other patients. He just wanted to stay in his room.

After weeks of pushing the therapy sessions to double the normal schedules, a slow gripping realization that he may never walk again settled in. He began to fight the battle of acceptance. Throughout his life, Gary always fought his way through (or around) to get what he wanted. This time, however, it wasn't happening. I was worried.

Laurie had been working with a fairer learning to trim hooves to earn money for school clothes. The job was hard on the back, but she loved doing it. For a break, we headed for the big city to see Gary and shop for her clothes. I surprised Laurie with tickets to see the rock group, Blood, Sweat, and Tears. The groups name seemed an appropriate reflection of all that we were enduring. While visiting Gary, someone broke into the car and stole our suitcase with all our clothes and my beautiful bracelet, the first gift I had received from my husband.

Laurie was furious, and being her father's daughter, she declared, "I'm coming next weekend with another suitcase—full of horse manure!"

We did come the next weekend but without the manure. We didn't find Gary in his room or in the cafeteria. We wandered around and finally entered the recreation room where we found him "wheelchair dancing" with that cute girl. Laurie and I both grinned. I was relieved. Gary fought the battle to accept his condition—and won!

The staff began to allow Gary home for the weekends. He, of course, wanted to stay, but the rehab doctors said no, not yet. After one very emotional weekend, I drove him back at the latest hour possible, and the orderly seemed quite gruff. As they turned to enter the elevator, I spotted a whiskey bottle in the orderly's pocket. Facing me, Gary's eyes pleaded like a hurt puppy's. In the next second, the elevator doors closed. My eyes brimming with tears, I walked quickly to the dark parking lot. A stiff wind dried my tears, and I fumbled with the keys before finally flinging myself into the seat of the car.

I always hated driving home late at night, but this time, the trip passed quickly as I rehearsed my intended, unwavering announcement to Gary's doctors that he be released. When I returned and delivered this speech, they initially objected, but Gary did come home with me.

When I rolled him into the house, Gary found the hospital bed positioned in our living room where he could see the pond through the huge floor-to-ceiling windows.

Laurie had hung a poster she made for him on the wall. In large letters, she had spelled out "TRUE GRIT," and friends signed their names around those words. Gary loved John Wayne movies and when Laurie went to see the movie and came home raving, as if John Wayne had just been discovered. Gary and I laughed and told her we had watched him on the screen when we were in school. Her mouth dropped open, and she looked at us incredulously.

I had carefully stocked the kitchen with Gary's favorite foods. A tray of medications and cigarettes sat at his bedside. There was also a folder of instructions and many prescriptions for medications and catheters. Our dogs picked up on the excitement and were so hilarious, we had to shoo them outside.

"I'm home. I'm really home!" Gary said with a grin. "After five long months, I'm really home."

"You're home...finally," I replied. "But you look tired. Let's call off visitors for a few days, okay?"

"Okay," he agreed with relieved and willing eyes.

Gary gazed at the white onyx stones covering our walls and fireplace.

"Remember how we used to sit by a roaring fire with all the lights out and pick out shapes and faces in the stone formations?" he asked.

"I sure do," I answered. That seemed like an eternity ago, but in the days ahead, Gary would have time to search the face of each wall inch by inch again.

Our driveway curved around the house to the lower level, where doors entered the garage and the recreation room. The main level was accessed by climbing spiral stairs outside or by entering the recreation room and following an intriguing stone stairway that wound around a huge central column of white onyx. This column contained four fireplace openings, one on each floor.

On the main level, a suspended stairway hugged that same stone column and led to the master bedroom.

From there, you'd enter a small hidden stairway in the fireplace wall. It curved around like real castle steps and led to a deck concealed by a false roof, with another fireplace to enjoy barbecuing under the stars or sunshine. Our house was built into the hill, so Gary entered the back way through the sliding glass doors into the living room. *This* room would be his living quarters as both wings and bathrooms were impossible or extremely difficult to maneuver, due to his bulky wheelchair.

While watching the moon one glorious evening, we had observed the first moon walk on TV from our rooftop hideaway. We enjoyed nights spent in the barn, hoping to see a new foal born, friends fishing for bass and parties—lots of parties. Gary and I began to realize this castle home was not for us now and, in time, would learn that it *never* really was.

As we settled into our daily routine at home, our eyes began to focus and readjust differently to the world around us. We haltingly began the journey of assessing our past, our objectives, our desires, and most painfully, our mistakes. Things that we once held dear, like little sacred gods, became worthless under the scrutiny of our new eyes. Mentally, we began to jettison these useless gods into the junk heap and started our search for something better.

It wasn't all easy. The unexpected patience that surfaced in Gary during his hospital stay would at times be strained to the extreme in the day-to-day stress of learning to cope with his new limits. He was an adventurer at heart, and his physical limitations could not squelch that boldness. I was an adventurer of sorts too. After all, I married him! For us, life was to become more of a collection of actions and experiences than a collection of things.

Gary's thirst for speed and thrills did not disappear with the loss of his legs. I fingered the photo, the last one taken of Gary standing. He was holding up a large-mouth bass snagged from our pond, a triumphant grin on his face. This would not be the last fish Gary would catch, I was sure of that. Tightness gripped my chest as I suddenly recalled a night before the accident; it was the last time the two of us had shared physical intimacy of man and wife. With tension in our marriage, even that had become tarnished and mechanical. It loomed more precious now.

"Poor me" never surfaced in Gary's attitude. I think that would have been the most difficult reaction for me to handle. Except for brief pangs of sadness in the knowledge that we would have to leave our castle on the hill, I didn't shoulder the burden of self-pity either. Our shared ability to adjust and our sense of humor must have been God's gift to soften the harshness of lessons in our joint life. Oh God, what now?

CHAPTER 3

Memories have a dance of their own
at times so sharp and clear.
Then again, they fade away,
even those we hold most dear.
Kindly time will soften edges
of those that cut so deep.
Then bring us laughter and sunshine
on days our music sleeps.
We are making memories every day
with all our minutes hold.
If we could only see the time
when present days are told.

We watched the midday sun reflect millions of dancing lights across the pond as Gary and I talked and tried to unravel the tangled skein of our lives.

Sipping a mug of hot tea, Gary spoke, sighed, and quietly said, "We need a good parcel of land, but a smaller house that is wheelchair accessible."

I studied his face, feeling his pain and sense of helplessness. We had high hopes and dreams of better health, but the day-to-day struggle was enormous. Life was now filled with pressure spots, kidney infections, visits to the doctor, trips to physical therapists, and financial disasters.

"You're right," I answered. "A simple house, easy to maintain, rooms that are open, with hard smooth floors for your wheelchair, along with some pasture land." There was never a thought of giving up our horses. They were part of the family.

I silently gathered our tea mugs to wash them, and from the kitchen window, I watched Laurie riding Hooligan. Her blond hair flying in the wind, body in perfect harmony with the dark steed beneath her, they seemed to paint a picture of freedom riding across the open field. Hooligan, alias L. F. Dhu Julio, was a misleading name. He was a horse to love with his gallant spirit, gentle ways, and a heart to please. Because of his outrageous habit of sticking his tongue out to be rubbed, he was not popular with the judges in a horse show, but we didn't mind. Hooligan was foaled in a pasture and injured very young from a kick in the mouth. His previous owners had rubbed his cut tongue to heal the injury, and to him, it was a caress.

Now, as I watched Laurie and Hooligan, tears flowed. I remembered Gary and Laurie riding together. The tears dried along with the dishes, and I had to smile, thinking back to a "great race day." Gary had challenged Laurie to a race up our long lane and back. Laurie was to ride Penny, our Quarter Horse, and Gary would be astride Hooligan. Penny would, of course, be ahead on the way up, but Gary was sure the stamina of the Arabian would win the race on the home stretch.

Laurie shocked me as they went out the door. She winked and whispered, "Penny's in season, and Hooligan won't pass her tail." Penny did jump ahead at the start, but coming home, Gary lay up on Hooligan's neck, whispered in his ear, and flew down the stretch to win.

Flustered but laughing, Laurie slid off Penny's sweating sides and gasped, "What did you say to him?"

Gary just winked and grinned.

The sharp ringing of the phone interrupted my reminiscing. Gary answered and told me it was his friend, Dave Jamesen, inviting him to go for a ride. Dave graciously offered to drive Gary around to look for land to build a new home.

"Great, Dave. I'd love it," he said.

Gary was grateful for friends who would wrestle the wheelchair and take him away for a while. So was I.

Our days were full, and Laurie was busily involved in school activities. Signing the permission slip for a field trip to Cheff Center, a therapeutic horseback riding school for the challenged in Augusta, Michigan, I had not a clue what this was going to mean in my life. Coming home the day of the excursion, Laurie burst in the door full of excitement, talking a mile a minute.

"Dad, it was great! I helped a paraplegic like you ride a horse! Oh, Mom, I loved it! I would like to do this for a career. You can go there and train to become an instructor," she bubbled.

Laurie had never been much for horse shows, except jumping. To her, the showing depended too heavily on the judges' personal tastes. But this new aspect of horseback riding captivated her heart.

"I wish we lived near Cheff. I could volunteer for the classes," Laurie went on. "If you could just see it, all types of disabilities and everyone riding and having a ball. I want you to go there with me, Dad! You would love it!"

She could not understand her father's lack of enthusiasm. He was struggling and just not well enough at that time to be thrilled at the prospect of riding again. Instead, his mind was focused on the problems swirling around us.

In the middle of all this, Laurie fixed her sights on another, more immediate dream—Africa. A teacher at her school was recruiting students for a six-week study tour in Kenya, under the American Institute for Foreign Study, to take place in the summer of 1972.

"Please, Mom, Dad. I really want to go. There are quite a few going from our school. It would be *very* educational! Besides, my teacher is going as one of the chaperones, and she taught in Africa. It will be great!"

Gary and I were unsure of our feelings about the trip. We both had traveled, but Africa? It would be a long way from us for our fifteen-year-old daughter.

Gary and I began discussing Laurie's request after supper when Laurie was in her room. We began reminiscing over some of our own adventurous trips, one in particular. Entertaining our best dealers, several years earlier, we took them on a free trip to Acapulco, which was a delightful success. While we were there, Gary complimented me on making sure everyone had a wonderful time. In fact, he was so pleased that he had a special surprise for me.

"I've made arrangements for us to stay longer," he announced with a big Cheshire cat grin.

"Wonderful! I'll call Mom and Dad and tell them they can keep Laurie a little longer. I know they won't mind," I said happily. I envisioned myself lounging on the beach under a palm tree, completely relaxed.

In his next breath, Gary enthusiastically informed me, "We're going down to the jungle to hunt!"

Turning white right through my tan, I gasped. "I should have known. I can *hardly* wait!"

We flew in a small plane that included Scotch tape over holes in the plane's body, and a pilot and guide who did not speak English. In the middle of the instrument panel was a compass that the pilot would bang with his fist every once in a while as we flew between mountain peaks. Through clenched teeth, I said, "Thank you for this wonderful surprise!"

"You're very welcome," Gary sweetly replied as he pushed his cigarette stub out a hole someone forgot to tape.

After what seemed like a forever flight, we finally approached our unknown destination. As we circled, I peered out a side window at the clearing in the dense jungle growth. Below, I could make out a tiny village perched on the edge of a wide winding river, small huts hugging its banks. The pilot made a few passes over the open space in front of the village to clear out natives, animals, and chickens. That treetop-brushing landing was one of the quickest I ever experienced, but at least, we were on the ground.

Tumbling out, we stared at curious eyes, which stared right back at us. Everyone but Gary and I began talking. Gary just grinned, and the village men grinned. I searched the crowd for a woman to grin at, but none appeared.

There were handshakes, pats on the back, and a party of sorts began. The men would demonstrate their strength by picking up a heavy object, and then, they would point to Gary. He, in turn, would pick up something heavier. Everyone laughed, and this went on for some time. Suddenly, Gary grabbed a large ax and held it in front of him, his arm out straight as he gripped the upright ax by the handle. Slowly, he tilted the blade down toward his nose, not quite touching it. A wave of noisy approval rolled through the crowd of village men.

Then several of the men tried to duplicate the trick but stopped before the ax was anywhere near their faces. I was never sure if they were truly afraid, or being polite, by letting Gary do something they couldn't.

I was still scanning the bush for women when the pilot signaled it was time for him to leave. So we unloaded our supplies and watched the plane barely miss the treetops on takeoff. Villagers then led us to our open-air room under a thatched roof. Hanging our tropical hammocks on each side, I asked Gary, "Where do I go to the bathroom?"

Smiling, he replied, "I have no idea, but I'll find out!" He retrieved our Spanish book but eventually discovered that the villagers did not speak the same version of Spanish explained in our book. Finally, Gary resorted to sign language. They, in turn, made us to understand that the bathroom was behind any bush. I had to hike quite a distance before finding a clean bush.

Walking down to the river, we gazed at a row of dugout boats with brand-new motors on them. Gary was excited because someone told him that we would go down the river to hunt in one of these. However, that was not to be, as an archaeological expedition had come across the river from Guatemala and rented all the boats the villagers would spare.

While Gary was upset by the lack of available boats, I was stunned to realize that the far shore across the river was Guatemala! I'd had no idea that we were that far down in the Mexican jungle. The archeologists showed up and loaded the boats. We stood there and talked with them, a little excitedly since they spoke English. When they shoved off, we turned and went dejectedly up the bank to our jungle abode.

I opened a small overnight case that I had thrown some things into while trying to decide what to stuff in an airport locker until our return. Pinned beside the mirror in the case was a pair of dangling rhinestone earrings. When I glanced up, I found myself looking into a beautiful small face, with one flaw of crossed eyes, looking into mine. The child smiled, and we both laughed. The earrings fascinated her, so I put them on her and let her look in the mirror. We laughed again, and my heart sang at the wonderful trust of children.

She reached up to remove the earrings, but I grinned and shook my head. I wanted her to keep them. The girl leaped up and sprinted home to show off her gift. I thought of my blond Laurie at home with her grandparents, and a sharp pang of longing shot through me. I could almost feel her hand in mine and wished she were on my lap right then. I sighed. At least, I knew there were women somewhere nearby.

Getting into a tropical mood, Gary and I went to bed early. We lay there, listening to the rustling trees and hoping for a good night's sleep. As evening twilight yielded to a rich, dark night, we began to relax.

"Isn't this great?" Gary asked enthusiastically. "Just listen to all the night sounds. I bet we'll sleep well tonight!"

Suddenly radios came on, blaring loudly.

"What on earth?" I cried.

Now we guessed what was in some of the crates unloaded from the plane for the locals. Covering our ears to block out the loud heaving of drunken men, we did not get to sleep until early morning.

I awoke and stole a glance in Gary's direction. He was still sleeping. His hammock had broken in the night, and although his feet were in the air, his head was on the ground. A dog was curled up beside him, and a chicken was roosting on his legs. When I burst out laughing, he groaned awake, surveyed the situation, and joined in my laughter.

Smoke rose from the huts, and the flap-flap sound of women making tortillas drifted our way. Our guide came and built a fire for us, then fixed us breakfast with our supplies. Gary was invited to tour through one of the local homes, but I, as a woman, was excluded. I discovered this would be the rule in most situations.

A short man dressed in white pants and shirt, but sporting a large gun on his belt, ran the village. Gary tried to make it clear that we had come to hunt. I had fun watching him pantomime what he wanted to say. At last, plans were made to go into the jungle and hunt for their small deer, but I was not to be included. Gary acted out that I would go where he did. They vehemently shook their heads no. My husband held his ground, and they eventually agreed to make me an exception. I was officially part of the hunting party.

We walked and walked until I suspected we were walking in circles. But finally, we reached a deep ravine spanned by a narrow log. Everyone tripped across easily, including Gary, and then, my turn came.

I was scared, but Gary coaxed me, "Come on, Sandy. It's easy."

I took a deep breath and began to inch my way over.

When I had crossed about a third of the way, Gary yelled, "Don't look down!" Of course, I immediately did, lost my balance, and toppled off the log.

Looking up from a bush full of thorns, I again thanked him for this special gift. Yes, there was a *thorn* bush in the jungle...just waiting for me! The men rescued me and helped me to the other side of the ravine, and Gary plucked the thorns from *my* other side.

Gary bagged his deer, and we hiked back to the village. I watched with feelings dangerously close to revenge as the locals told and retold the story of my disaster. I may not have understood the lingo, but I had no trouble translating the fingers walking in the air and then falling down, followed by loud peals of raucous laughter.

Rain fell every day in the jungle. The day our plane was to arrive for us, we gave our remaining supplies to the village. However, our plane didn't show up. It didn't come the next day either or the next. Gary kept pointing to the sky as a question, but everyone shrugged and gestured that there was too much rain. They did not return our canned food, but they did give sun-dried meat and a root that tasted a little like sweet potatoes when we boiled it.

If the weather cleared at all, the men took machetes and cut sugar cane. One afternoon, they came to our quarters, which we finally realized was their barn. Although the sides were open, above our hammocks, there was a floor under the roof. This was where the local bachelor slept at night.

The men brought in their mule and hooked him up to a grinding wheel, and then ground sugar cane to prepare it for boiling. A large fire was started, and the ground cane went into a huge pot. When the cane had boiled sufficiently, the men turned over the chicken roosts. Beneath them were the sugar molds, which they simply brushed off before pouring in the heavy mixture to cool. That night, we drank coffee with the dark brown sugar in it. It was amazingly good.

The bachelor sang while he worked, and his voice was magnificent. I kept thinking that if he were back in the States, he could be another Caruso. Many nights while we were in our hammocks, his rich voice would float down from his sleeping place above as he counted in Spanish numbers, and we would do the same in English for him.

Every morning when we awoke, the first thing we would check was the weather. Was it raining?

One dawn, I woke up to hear Gary gleefully shouting, "It's not raining!"

"It's raining on my side," I replied.

"How can that be?" Gary shot back.

"I don't know. I just know that there's water dripping down on my hammock," I said. Suddenly, the explanation for the "rain" hit me; the upstairs tenant had rolled over and was relieving himself over the side. His urine was dribbling down on my hammock! I immediately felt ill.

I couldn't stand the uncleanness any longer! I had not had a genuine bath since we got here. After the episode in the hammock, I was definitely going to wash. Sneaking down to the river, I stepped into one of the boats and crawled out to the end farthest in the water. Stripping off my upper clothes, I dipped a rag in the water and began to scrub myself. Washing felt heavenly. But as I turned around, I glanced up the bank. There sat a smiling row of village men, watching. By that time, I simply didn't care anymore. Bathing became more important than modesty. In fact, I was beginning to wonder if the plane was ever coming back.

I trudged back to our quarters and tearfully hurled my feelings at Gary.

"We're never going to get out of here!" I cried. "No one at home even knows where we are."

Gary reacted like a character in a dime novel. He grabbed me and shook me and said, "I've never got you into anything I couldn't get you out of!"

With more tears, I replied, "This might be a first!"

Whimpering, I took Gary's canvas shoes down to the bank to wash them. I was muttering to myself as I scrubbed, but I abruptly halted when I heard the sound of a motor—an airplane! Running back to camp, I collided with my confident hero gone mad.

"Grab this! Get that! We're not going to let that pilot get away without us!" Gary shouted.

I dashed back to the riverbank to fetch his shoes, just in time to see a boatload of grinning villagers from up river paddle off. My husband's shoes were gone.

When the little plane touched down, Gary wasted no time loading our small bundles into it. We waved good-bye, skimmed the treetops on takeoff, and headed back to civilization with Gary wearing flip-flops.

Later, finally able to retrieve our musty-smelling clothes from the lockers at the airport, we boarded a plane back to the states and collapsed into our seats. Gary poked me with his elbow and began gesturing, as if to tell me something in sign language. Momentarily disoriented, he had fallen back into jungle-communication mode.

"I speak English," I reminded him.

His face turned red, and I howled good and loud, not caring about the startled stares from other passengers.

Now though, back in our castle, despite our frustrations, we held our sides as we laughed and relived this whole account. Then Gary became more solemn, saying, "But remember, by the time we landed in Chicago, you were very ill and very unpopular when they had to quarantine the plane."

"I know. We—and a lot of other passengers—missed our connecting flights. Then I spent a miserable night in a hotel room, just wishing I could die."

The next day, I felt better, and we thought it was dysentery, but as the months went by, more and more strange symptoms appeared, and I finally ended up in the hospital. It took a while, but it was finally diagnosed as Reiter's disease. The doctor had seen only one other case, in Puerto Rico, when he was in the service.

"If you hadn't taken me down to that jungle—" I began.

"Oh, it was all that lemonade you insisted on drinking in Acapulco!" Gary laughed.

I observed Gary's catheter bag needed emptying, and as I took care of that chore, I thought to myself how many things could happen to Laurie…in Africa.

We talked and talked. Then sitting in the darkened living room, we finally agreed that life is to be lived as an adventure. The next summer, we agreed that Laurie could go to Africa. I sat quietly and thoughtfully late into the night. "Oh God, we love her so."

CHAPTER 4

Life is still an adventure,
and the path's becoming steep.
Sharp stones loom large
in fields that we must reap.
We loudly sing our song of hope,
but yearn for quiet peace.
Our awkward, halting, tired dance
seeks something out of reach.
Will our strong and stoic hearts
mend us where we bleed?
Or is this dance a mask
that hides the greater need?

Summer submitted to fall. Then quickly, we were in the leading edge of winter.

"Sandy, my leg bag is leaking!" came the cry from outside.

This is the call I would hear for years to come. This time, Gary was in an all-terrain vehicle, a little six-wheeler. He had been wheeling all over the property and spinning doughnuts in the fresh snow. I ran outside, helped him into the wheelchair, and took him inside.

After I stripped him down and redid everything, he was back outside and at it again. He took the indignity of urinating into a bag strapped to his leg in stride.

The day he brought the six-wheeler home, he took Laurie for a ride and headed straight for the pond.

"Dad!" she screamed, thinking he had lost his senses as they splashed into the water.

Gary laughed and yelled, "Hang on!"

The little red amphibious machine slowly putted around but couldn't get out because of the icy buildup around the edge of the pond. Friends were there, so they hauled them out. Some things never change.

With the onset of winter, I wanted to check the deck on the roof one last time for anything left up there. Emerging from the dark stairway and onto the deck, I was exhilarated by the cool air and pristine look of the snow-covered countryside. The scene before me was beautiful, and I felt a soft throb of pity for myself as I faced the prospect of leaving it. I loved this hill. To the south was a three-acre pond, almost a small lake, fed by Sheep Creek. Beyond were wooded hills said to hold remnants of the Old Daniel Boone Trail.

To the north, you could see far off, even the glittering water tower of a town miles away in another state. I sighed, wishing I could see into the future. My eyes finally lowered to the stable below and our long lane. All was quiet, but in my mind, pictures played about, one after another: Laurie driving her pony Red Whisky down the lane, bringing home her funny little Polish chicken, Phyllis Diller, on her lap. Phyllis couldn't see well with all those feathers hanging in her face, so she tended to get lost a lot.

I could still picture Laurie sneaking over the fence to "steal" a watermelon after our dear neighbor, Mr. Judson, said with a wink in his eye, "There are lots of extra watermelons, and some really big ones by your fence." It wasn't really stealing, of course, since everybody knew that everybody knew. And that melon had sure tasted delicious.

I remembered all three of us washing two filthy angora goats that Gary had seen fit to bring home. When we were finished, those two goats bolted and ran for the hills, never to be seen again, even after countless horseback treks to find them.

My attention was drawn once more to the lane, where a car was slowly making its way toward the house. I reluctantly stepped back indoors, pulled the heavy door shut, and picked my way down the narrow passageway to the bedroom. Drawing in a deep breath, I quickly descended the stairs to greet whomever was coming.

It turned out to be Gary's friend, Dave. He had dropped by to say, "Let's go for an outing, Gary."

Oh, what sweet words for us both! My time of being alone on the hill was long since over. These days I constantly knew where my husband was every *minute* every *day!* Speak of togetherness!

Gary and Dave were again going to look at a parcel of land we were considering buying. Laurie was ecstatic about the idea, as the property bordered the land and home of her boyfriend, Kent. Kent's father was our veterinarian, and like us, his family also raised horses.

The property was located on a winding and hilly dirt road. There was no dwelling on it, but lots of woods and pastureland. We finally decided it was right for us.

Gary was regaining strength, and we talked much about our needs but still only physical and material ones. We sometimes mentioned God in our conversations but in an abstract way about what he would want us to do. We did not understand or know how to depend on God. We did not attend church or read God's word. Fighting through each crisis or trial with a cheery can-do attitude, we struggled along on our own strength.

When the castle on the hill sold, a changed life began for us. With nowhere to go, we moved the horses and Ali Baa-Baa to our new property. Our little Mop dog, Trinket, went to live with my mother, and the rest of us moved to an extremely small trailer home my sister Jo let us use—and it was culture shock. Like us, the dogs experienced the stress of moving also, but their antics and faithfulness were a comfort to us.

The hospital bed was placed crossways in front of the trailer. That was where Gary was forced to stay when inside. From big, big, big we went to tiny, tiny, tiny. But we were grateful for a place to live.

We began sketching ideas for our new home, and everything leaned toward rustic. With the help of friends, we tore down a one-hundred-year-old barn that was headed for destruction. Working carefully, we salvaged the beautiful beams and wonderful poplar siding. Unable to join in the actual work, Gary spun around the site in his six-wheeler calling out encouragement, "You can lift that. It's not that heavy. Just grab and lift!"

His enthusiasm worked because later, it took four carpenters to lift the same beams that two friends had loaded on the trailer.

A sudden scream stabbed the activity.

"Mom! I stepped on a nail!" Laurie yelled. The wound was deep and required a doctor visit, along with a tetanus shot. Despite this added trauma and all the extremely heavy work, somehow, we managed to get the old barn dismantled. It was a pleasure to know the still-beautiful beams and wood would be used again. They certainly blended into the rustic décor of our new home.

Early in spring, the builders set to work on our home. While Gary talked with the workmen, I spent hours walking the hilly woods and fields, my heart lifting and feeling lighter than it had in many months. Nature's healing balm began to tug at me and gently turn my thoughts to God. There were whispers in the spring wind and a fresh emergence of hope.

Along with others going to Africa later that spring, Laurie began lessons with two exchange students at a local college to learn Swahili. For the two of us, the Monday night ritual became Swahili lessons, and while I waited the hour for her, a chance for me to swat tennis balls against a brick wall.

We were anxious for the house to be finished. The move to the trailer had been a nightmare. We stored belongings everywhere, and I wondered if we would ever get everything back and in order.

Laurie's sixteenth birthday arrived in March. "Isn't it great that I can drive? It will help a lot with my activities and the trip each day to care for the horses," she said. She was thrilled.

"Yes, it will," I agreed but with feelings of apprehension.

Spring seemed to run a relay and too quickly handed its days to summer. Laurie was well into preparing for her adventure to Africa.

At 2:00 a.m. on a July morning, the Kenya Safari gang started out for New York City in a violent thunderstorm. The group consisted of six other girls from school and one lone boy: Kent, Laurie's boyfriend. The three-car caravan experienced a somewhat difficult time staying together in the storm, but they did reach New York, where the students boarded a flight to London and at last to Nairobi for a six-week adventure.

After Laurie's departure, a subdued atmosphere settled over the tiny trailer.

"It seems strange without Laurie," Gary said softly.

"Yes, it does." I sighed, sad for me, but happy for her.

"I hope she has a wonderful time. You lectured her more than enough on how to use that camera and how to take care of it!" I snapped.

Gary didn't reply.

The carpenters working on our house had to deal with the animals that were still running all over the place. They had to watch the horses, or they might try to eat the paint from their cars. Ali Baa-Baa had a fascination for the stonemason and kept chasing him around the fireplace that divided the kitchen from the living area. Red Whiskey, our small red pony, knew instinctively when it was noon and would come ambling in to beg for a treat or part of some generous worker's sandwich.

There was an old rolled-up piece of wire fencing and railroad ties in one of the pastures. Two longtime friends, Henry and Jack, came to help us move them so the horses wouldn't get tangled in them. Their wives and I sat on a log to watch, while Gary gave directions. Ali Baa-Baa, who never missed a thing, came running to see what was going on. He leaned over to watch as the men picked up a railroad tie. The tie was big, heavy, and stuck. When it finally came loose, it struck Ali Baa-Baa under his chin. The two men didn't let go. They simply started walking away with it. Ali Baa-Baa stood for a minute, shook his head, and thought over what had just happened to him. In the next instant, the sheep lowered his head and broke into a run toward Jack, who had his back to him.

About that time, Jack happened to glance up and see Henry's eyes getting bigger. But before Henry could yell a warning—*pow!*—Ali rammed Jack in the seat.

All of us ladies tumbled off the log laughing, tears streaming down our faces. The men also shed some tears, but not from laughter. Believe it or not, we were not sued, and it was decided not to butcher Ali.

Something that had never held much importance in our lives now became a yearned for event...a letter. Specifically a letter from Africa, which took forever. Both Gary and I felt the allure of Africa, and before his accident, we had talked often about traveling there. The places Laurie would be seeing—Nairobi, Mombasa, Tsavo, Ngorongoro Crater, Olduval Gorge, and of course, the ever romantic sounding Mt. Kilimanjaro—seemed to convey excitement with their unique tones. We really envied Laurie.

One day, we received a letter from Laurie, asking us to call a number at a pay phone on the college grounds where she was taking classes as she was not allowed to call out. She wrote that she would be waiting on a certain day and time to hear from us. There was a problem, however, because the letter was so late. The appointed day was long past. Not knowing what to do, we tried the number at the correct hour each day. No one would answer, and Gary was quite distraught worrying that Laurie would think that we were so busy we had forgotten to call. Then one day, that precious familiar voice lifted the receiver on the pay phone!

"Hello, Dad? Dad! Yes, this is me. What's happened? Oh, Dad!"

There was a burst of tears on both ends of the line, which continued for most of the thirty-five minutes we talked. She had decided to visit the phone booth once more, and we connected. Father and daughter both knew how much they loved one another, in spite of their feisty disagreements. The days were measured from then on by when we would see her again.

At last, we were on our way to New York City to meet the plane carrying our precious daughter home. As it turned out, the plane was late because of an emergency stop for repairs after leaving Nairobi. So the group enjoyed an unscheduled thirteen hours on the Mediterranean island of Malta.

As Laurie came down the ramp into the airport, she burst into tears. "Dad, oh Dad, I'm sorry. I'm so sorry!"

"What's wrong? I can't understand you," Gary said, trying to hug her from the wheelchair.

"My film. Someone stole it in London while we were trying to change planes," she cried. "All of it…all my film, every picture I took. I bought a new purse and put it all in there, and it's gone!"

The story spilled out. She had been saying good-bye to Kent in London as he was staying behind to backpack through Europe. When she returned to collect her things to board the plane, her new purse was gone, and all her film with it.

"It's all right. It's all right. You're home," we both replied, hugging her close.

We took the girls to a hotel room to freshen up and rest before heading home. They jumped on the waterbeds and let off steam. The teacher, Jean Snyder, was flying back to Indiana, so Gary and I went to rent a tow bar for Jean's car, which we volunteered to tow behind our station wagon. We piled everyone into our car and began the trek for home. After six weeks in Africa, the girls showed a newfound fascination for American food and plastic straws at our first restaurant stop. By 1:30 a.m., we were home in Middlebury, Indiana.

Prince, our Collie, was so happy to see Laurie that he just fell apart along with us. Their relationship began years before when Laurie and her dad were visiting friends. Laurie was fascinated by their Tennessee walkers and wanted to ride one of them. They put her on, not telling her that they cantered like a rocking horse. She rode behind a large bush, and the horse emerged without her. Laurie stumbled out from the other side holding her arm.

"I think I sprained it," she said. One look told Gary it was broken. He drove her to the emergency room, and a doctor set it. Later, back home, Laurie began to talk about the beautiful Collie she had seen at our friends' house.

"He's a stray, Mom, and they really don't want him," Laurie begged. "He put up his paw exactly like Lassie on TV."

So Gary and Laurie drove back to our friends' house that same night, and Prince became part of our family. He loved Laurie, and the love was mutual. Now, back home from her African adventure, she buried her head in his beautiful ruff and hugged him close. All the animals loved her, and horses especially missed their workouts with her while she was gone.

We were anxious to hear everything about her trip. She brought home carvings, a zebra skin, a beautiful Masai blood gourd, and many other treasures and exciting tales.

Africa had not disappointed her. The first passionate point she made to us was, "I want to go back someday."

The sheer wonderment of the continent, the vastness, the people and animals, all captured a part of her. One never travels without broadening one's self, and we could easily see that changes had occurred in our daughter.

Laurie was also saddened by the realization that steady changes were taking place in that exotic land, including a disregard for its immense wealth of wilderness. We listened to stories of learning, of growing, and of just crazy fun with the safari gang. But most of all, Laurie talked about the people and the beauty she saw.

"Mom, I didn't expect Nairobi to be so modern or so big," Laurie mused. "I had a distorted view of Africa before. And although I loved it, I sure do appreciate my own country more."

Laurie twirled her hair around a forefinger. "You know, I loved London too. We were there such a short time, and I really want to go back."

"I hope you can, Laurie," I said with a smile. "There's so much to see in this old world."

Laurie sighed. "I know, and I love traveling—and books! I could spend a lot of money on both."

"I think you have," I commented with a grin.

She laughed. "Oh, Mom. Not nearly enough!"

Laurie shared some long talks with her dad, and father and daughter came to a better understanding of each other's views. I reminded Gary that he had always told Laurie to stand up for what she thought was right. As she grew older, I told him he would occasionally have to respect her opinions that were different from his. The combative currant that ran between these two softened. Through the years, I had observed that their many conflicts in opinion were fanned to a flame by their similar temperaments.

At the arrival home of everyone from Africa, the fall session of school had already begun. Laurie was rushed to get organized and back in the routine. She had a hard time coming down from the peak of excitement after the trip and getting back into her schoolwork. Stepping into the house one afternoon with tears in her eyes, she threw her books down.

"I gave my report today on the book *I Buried My Heart at Wounded Knee*. The class laughed at it. They just don't understand! Why don't they understand?"

"I don't know, Laurie, but I'm glad you do," I said quietly.

"You know, Mom, everybody at school is so concerned with themselves. It's easy for the kids to be really cruel. It seems kids should care about their friends, not try to impress them. I think there are a lot of really lonely kids suffering silently. I just hate it when you walk down the hall and greet someone, and they don't smile or speak. They act like you're not there…It makes me sick!"

"I know what you mean, Laurie."

"Well, I guess I've been guilty of it too," Laurie added thoughtfully.

"It's easy to get wrapped up in ourselves. Teenagers are searching and learning about themselves, so sometimes, when they're just being self-conscious, it comes out looking like they're stuck-up. Don't you think so?" I asked.

Laurie's blond head nodded in agreement, and her beautiful brown eyes softened. She made a delightfully charming picture in her yellow-patterned, soft-flowing dress. Laurie was small, but she inherited her father's straight back and solid bone structure. She was physically strong and athletic but definitely feminine. She seemed to exude certain electricity that was attractive but kept you a little on the edge. My daughter was growing up and pulling away. She was not a follower.

As she left the room, I remembered a time when at ten years old, she had stood firm. Gary and I were going through marital problems. I left his clothes on the doorstep and changed the locks. He lived in a motel for quite a few months.

During that time, Laurie came to me, standing straight, and looked me right in the eye to say, "I want you to know that no matter what happens, I love you and Daddy just the same."

There was no choosing sides with her! The crisis ended one night when Daddy called for a date, and a joyful little girl went home with both Mom and Dad.

Sitting in the corner of the sofa, I hugged my knees and thought back. What a steep road our marriage has traveled since then. What if we had tossed our vows out, along with our problems, and each searched for a new path for happiness? Where would I be? Where would Gary be? And Laurie? Would we have found happiness? Smiling, I sighed. I knew better. A soft gentle voice calling in my heart was speaking of joy, not mere happiness. I didn't fully understand yet, but a beckoning glimmer of truth tugged at me. Without realizing it, I began a new journey.

"God, I'm changing. God, I do not understand, but things are different. Open my heart to know. Help!"

CHAPTER 5

Through my crumbling ruins,
a vicious wind now blows,
Howling to the empty rooms
to kill all final hopes.
I feel it through the broken panes;
my lips are cold as ice.
"There's no hope here," I scream,
"just death, there is no life!"
Is this your killing wind, Lord?
Is sin or anger its source?
Am I broken for a reason,
or is fate the driving force?

It would soon be Christmas. We were finally in our new home and trying to finish up a lot of the inside work. The house was small but designed for Gary's wheelchair, and the stable was attached to the garage. Gary was excited about the freedom to wheel right through the garage into the stable and enjoy a new foal or visit an old friend.

My mother and my sister Josephine's family were coming for Christmas, and I was working around the clock to get things ready. Not receiving much help from Laurie, I took the opportunity to tell her so.

"You are *definitely* going overboard," she growled.

"I know!" I yelled. "It's my family!"

"So?" she shot back. "Are they coming to see us or this house?"

"Both," I screamed. "Now get busy!"

With only a few days to go, the workman finished putting in the black grouting on the brick floor in the entrance way. I think they observed my glazed eyes and felt the tension as I tried to smile calmly at one and all.

Trying to be helpful, they decided to clean up the floor when they were finished. One gentleman grabbed my water vac and swept up every leftover piece of grouting and dust. I was in the bedroom helping Gary. When I came out, I thought I saw smoke in the air, and then, I realized the vacuum was blowing a black film on everything. I yelled at the top of my lungs, and he shut the sweeper off.

Staggering around, I touched the white walls. The beautiful stucco Henry just finished was covered with a black, oily finish. The cupboards, the floor, the ceiling, the windows—everything! The workman quietly left, and I went sobbing to Gary.

"Don't get upset," he said cheerily.

"Don't get up upset? What do you mean don't get upset?" I spit out in staccato.

He sighed. "I'll call Henry."

The next day found me trying to put up our huge Christmas tree while Henry was washing, painting, and generally redoing the living room.

"I don't know what to do," I whined. "My tree is too big for the stand. I think I might have another one, but where *that* would be, I haven't a clue. Henry, I have to run to the store. I'll be back shortly."

When I returned, a triumphant and smiling Henry met me at the door.

"Don't worry about your tree. I have it fixed for you," he said in his lilting Spanish accent.

He led me to the living room where my tall tree was placed in a large plastic bucket full of mortar. The top was tied to a beam on the ceiling.

"When it hardens, you can untie it," he said proudly.

I just stood there in amazement.

"Well, I won't have to water it," I said weakly. I smiled at the grinning face and left to carry in the groceries. Putting things away, I peeked again at the tree and thought to myself, that sucker's sure going to be heavy to carry out of here!

Somehow, it all came together for Christmas Day. There was the traditional holiday food, presents, and laughter. The house was passable, and I thought everyone looked beautiful and festive. Kent was home from his travels and joined us for the merriment.

It seemed Laurie had taken particular care in choosing our gifts. I received much-desired cross-country skis, and her father was pleasantly surprised with a beautiful exotic wooden pen and pencil set. For herself, she only wanted a gift certificate to buy books.

The fun and flurry was over too quickly for all the time spent in preparation. Laurie and Kent walked out to the stable. Everyone began to gather up his or her gifts and groan about being full. Soon, the house was empty of its guests, and Gary looked very tired. I helped him undress and get into bed.

After Kent left and Laurie was also in bed, I stoked the fire and threw on another log. The sparks puffed upward, and the new wood began to crackle and spit, inviting me to sit down in the quiet darkened room.

The soft glow of the Christmas tree lights revealed the small nativity resting under the lowest evergreen branches. The gifts that hid it through the day were gone. Christmas day was passed in this house; not one sincere prayer was lifted to heaven, not one carol joyfully sung, no one reverently read the wondrous story of the Christ child—God becoming man—for us.

Tears filled my eyes as I remembered an earlier Christmas, my sister Jean playing the piano as the rest of the family gathered around to lift our happy voices and sing every carol in the book. Suddenly, I heard the TV go on in the bedroom.

Gary must not be able to sleep, I thought. The need to escape the blaring sound overwhelmed me, and I slipped out to the stable.

The horses did not seem surprised at their late-night visitor. A deep peaceful silence enveloped me, and I felt a sweet softness in the air. There was no Christmas glitter here. It was just a simple stable. I began to understand and felt a loving, gentle knocking at my heart's door.

The week after Christmas was pleasant. Our tree in the bucket was holding up well, so we left it towering over the living room in all its glory. Laurie and Kent were horseback riding whenever possible. They took turns on Hooligan and Mamacita. Laurie seemed to win no matter whom she was riding. This holiday race ended differently. Kent, on Mamacita, our Arab mare, won. Laurie fussed and fumed, mumbling something about Hooligan's leg. She didn't take losing very well.

We needed to move some hay from one barn to another, so right after the New Year, on the second of January, we began. Loading a hay wagon, Laurie and I worked hard and fast. Unloading was easier, but it still needed to be stacked. We did make it fun with competition and kidding. Finishing late in the afternoon, I began supper. Dave stopped by to eat with us, and later in the evening, Kent's parents, Mary and Bill, came by for a visit.

Laurie asked, "May I go down and visit with Kent?"

"No, it's too late," I explained.

"Please, I won't stay long."

"No, you can see him tomorrow."

"But why not?"

"No!"

Mary and Bill left, and I began to help get Gary into bed. Laurie went to her room but came back out.

"Mom, I would like to sleep on the couch and look at the tree for a while, okay?"

"Sure...It *is* a beautiful tree, isn't it?"

A few minutes later, Laurie said, "Mom, I've got a terrible headache. I need an aspirin or something."

Laurie finally settled down, and I fell into bed beside Gary. He seemed unusually tired and quiet for the talkative mood he was in earlier that evening. He did remind me to put the Christmas nuts away, so Duke couldn't get into them. We had, on occasion, awakened to a shell-strewn floor and empty nut bowl. It was amazing that our Great Dane could crack the hardest nuts with his big jaws, and then pick out the tiniest nutmeats. I groaned and pulled myself out of bed, checked out the nuts, told Laurie good night, and again crawled back in bed.

Hours later, I awoke with a start. There was an awful sound coming from somewhere in the house. It sounded like one of the dogs might be sick. Certainly something was wrong. I slipped out of bed, trying not to wake Gary. Running into the living room, I realized the noise was coming from the sofa.

Laurie looked asleep, but she was breathing with a loud rasping sound. I shook her, but there was no response. I grabbed her shoulders and raised her up, screaming for Gary to wake up and call for help. Trying again and again to revive her, I grasped the fact that she was in a coma and probably dying.

I screamed again, "Gary call the ambulance. Laurie is dying!"

"I have, and the Middlebury ambulance will not come! We are not in their territory," he yelled.

He then called the Hankins's residence. "Bill, please come and help us! Laurie is sick and dying! Help us get her to the hospital!"

Silently and swiftly, the color drained from the limp body of our daughter as Bill and Kent burst through the door. Bill scooped her up in his arms and carried her to his car. He got her in the back seat and gave mouth-to-mouth resuscitation. Gary had pulled the wheelchair over to the bed, made it to the sink in the bathroom, grabbed his leg bag, put it on, and then dressed in a matter of minutes. He came wheeling out to the car, and Kent picked him up and slid him in the front seat with me. Kent drove the few miles to the Bristol Fire Station while Bill kept working on her. Laurie was quickly put in an ambulance, and it screamed off.

We were shuffled into a police car and headed for the Elkhart Hospital, but before we could make it there, the dreaded message fell from the police radio like burning coals on my ears…

DOA. Dead on arrival.

Feeling no need to continue toward the hospital, the police offered to drive us home.

My world began to spin. I gripped the seat as a deep scream of agony pushed against my chest, but no sound came from my lips. I felt like a weight from hell was crushing the breath from my body and soul. Gary remained quiet as the car turned and delivered its broken passengers home in the first breaking of morning light.

As we slowly entered the house, I thought I couldn't bear to look over toward the sofa. When I was trying to wake her, I knew Laurie was really gone when the color drained from her face. I didn't want to see it again in my mind, but I would…many times over.

Seeing something on the floor, I bent over and picked up one of the flowered cotton napkins from the dinner the night before. Laurie must have used it to wipe her forehead. It was still damp with perspiration. Did she have a high fever? Why didn't she call us?

I clutched it to my chest, crying uncontrollably.

How could this be? What was the cause? How can we go on? Nothing matters now! Oh God, why Laurie?

"Why couldn't it have been me?" Gary cried. "*Why couldn't it have been me*? Look at me, what good am I?"

I couldn't even think how to answer him. I just stared at the still lit Christmas tree and the tiny lights on the deck railing through the front window. It was then I noticed the sketchbook on the table beside the sofa. I picked it up and opened it to the only drawing it contained. A chill ran through me as I stared at the silhouette of a young girl, head back, arms close to her body, with curved lines streaming from her to show her rising upward. I felt suddenly frozen.

Oh God, could Laurie have taken her own life? But why?

Gary and Kent went to tell my mother. I couldn't go… I just couldn't face her with the news. Mother was stunned and overwhelmed with grief. Laurie had been more than a granddaughter. She was her friend and confidant. Laurie always showed special concern and love for Mother and all elderly people. She had time for them as so few young people do.

Moving through the following days in a fog, we all managed to go on. The autopsy showed Laurie died of natural causes…specifically fulminating hyper acute bacterial or viral pulmonary infection. A virus, which doctors assumed she contracted in Africa, overtook her when she was tired. It perforated her esophagus, and she drowned in her own fluids. It is not a common occurrence, and I was told if we had made it to the hospital before she died, isolating the virus would have taken too much time to save her. There was relief knowing her death was not caused by suicide. I could not picture Laurie wanting to take her own life, but I knew many young people today think of it and do it.

We were brought to our knees, our hearts broken, and we moved as if in a dream. We looked at the world through our broken windows of pain, their jagged edges cutting us to the quick of our being. We smile at others passing by, but inside, there was just this howling and cold wind that turned us to ice.

For the first time, the question tore at our every waking moment: *why?* The funeral arrangements were made, Laurie's school friends created the beautiful service, Laurie's favorite songs were played, and standing before her daisy covered casket, I tucked her precious book *I Buried My Heart at Wounded Knee* beside her.

Staring at my beautiful, young daughter looking like she was asleep, I prayed she would forgive me. Just weeks before, in a discussion about death and funerals, she had revealed her vehement dislike of the general tradition of people filing by to see the deceased.

"I think it's barbaric, and if I should die, don't do it!" she said, flashing her dancing brown eyes at me.

I smiled then, thinking it would be a choice of hers in reverse, probably for me. Now as I stood there, I knew she would understand. Her grandmother had to see her, to face the fact that she was gone. I needed to see her, just as all her schoolmates and friends needed to see her. Kent needed to see her. We knew it was just her shell, but we needed to say good-bye and try to understand why.

Good-bye?

There was no chance to say good-bye. No illness that was known, no time. She was just gone. Friends were more than kind. My dear friend Marie came and spent that first night with us, afraid of what I might do. I needed her but could not really convey my thoughts. She slept on the sofa in front of the deck windows, and the small Christmas lights wound around the railings flicked off and on several times. Marie sat up and watched until they stopped and quietly said, "Good-bye, Laurie."

Gary maintained a calm exterior, but inside, he was sinking fast. He tried to control his tears when visitors came, but his face was strained, and he was weakening.

One night, he called out, "Sandy, I think I have a nose bleed. Will you help me?"

I rushed into his room, and when I turned on the light, I was shocked to see his head lying in a pool of blood. I cleaned him up, changed the sheets, and we began to apply cold compresses. It would lessen some, but soon, his nosebleed would start again to flow quite heavily.

In the morning, I announced, "I'm calling the doctor. Something has to be done now!"

Gary argued, "It will stop today I'm sure."

"Well, I'm not, and you have lost an immense amount of blood."

Dr. Unsucker came, and after seeing Gary, he said, "He needs to go into the hospital and have the blood vessels cauterized right away." We admitted Gary, and the procedure was done. The flow continued, and it was done again, and again, the flow continued. They were giving Gary blood intravenously, but the nosebleed would not stop.

"Mrs. Weatherwax, Gary wants to die, and he will unless he makes up his mind not to," Dr. Unsucker told me softly.

Each day's visit was the same. Gary kept his face turned to the wall and remained silent. Sitting alone that night, I prayed, "Please, dear God, help him see I need him. We need each other."

The next morning when I entered his room, I felt the difference immediately. Gary turned and looked at me with still dark and somber eyes, but there was a slight curve of a smile on his lips.

"I guess we still have each other, right?" he said slowly.

I ran and threw my arms around him, buried my head in his chest, and through tears, my muffled reply was, "Yes!"

Once again, Gary came home. We pushed on through the wall of days before us. Kent was suffering too. We all shared the loss, and Kent moved in with us for a while, so we could give support to one another. He was a delightful rush-ahead-and-stumble young man. Kent's enthusiasm for life was great, but in his hurry, he was just a little accident-prone. His engaging grin and great sense of humor soon began to surface again to benefit us all. He had his moments though. And after I heard "Born to be Wild" on the highest decibel our stereo could manage—over and over—I thought I might go wild myself.

Gary and I were reevaluating our life yet again. One of the excuses humans have for collecting things is to pass them down to their children. We now could cross off that reason. We searched for other reasons…reasons for our lives.

I sat in Gary's room and watched the melting snow from the roof drop past the windowpane. The TV was off, and Gary was unusually silent.

"You know, a parent's ego and identity can really be wrapped up in their children," I offered. "I feel stripped."

He said nothing.

"I have been thinking. I would like to do something in Laurie's honor…or as a memorial to her. Something for someone else. What do you think?" I tried again.

Another scoop of snow fell as the sun came out brighter. Gary finally responded with an ardent, "You're right!"

Then, the phone rang.

Gary's voice told me it was one of his friends, and I got up to leave.

"Just a minute, Sandy. There's a young girl, daughter of my friend. She would like to come out and ride the horses…Exercise them for us. Is that okay with you?"

I stuck my head back in the door, "Sure, we'll see how she can ride though. I'm not putting just anyone on our horses."

He grinned. "I know."

I went to the sink and the dirty dishes and began to dream again.

Oh God, I want to have meaning in my life I feel cold and bare. So many things seem useless Mend us

CHAPTER 6

God's gift of exquisite beauty
comes dancing on the wind.
Streamlined muscles ripple,
tiny hoofs beat out a rhythm.
Proud head and ancient lineage
held high with nostrils flared
Mane thick and furled like a flag
blowing free in rarefied air.
The Arabian stallion comes calling
from the deserts of long ago,
With strength and courage of heart
that you and I long to know.

I watched Hooligan go through his paces with a graceful and joyful attitude.

However, there was a difference. Replacing the familiar figure astride with the flying blond hair, there was now a small girl with a mane of black hair to match Hooligan's own. Her hands were wonderfully gentle on the reins, but firm. Jykla had arrived. The animals were won over immediately with her quiet and calm demeanor.

It was early morning, and I was in Gary's bedroom. He was still in bed reading the paper.

"I'm thrilled we have someone to exercise our horses," I chattered away to Gary as I folded clothes. I had a little something else I wanted to throw in but didn't know just how to approach it.

"Mmm…ahuh. She's great," he mumbled while trying to read.

"I think we should talk to her about starting a horseback riding school for the handicapped. That's what Laurie wanted to do. What do you think?"

The paper dropped, and I began stacking clothes, not daring to look at him.

He said, "You've been hinting around for some time now. You really want to do this, don't you?"

"Yes, I do!" I finally looked him in the eye. "I think Jykla would be a perfect instructor. Let's talk to her, okay?"

Soon Jykla, Gary, and I were caught in a rushing wave of confidence and enthusiasm for this project we thought of as Laurie's Dream. Remembering Laurie's excitement when she was telling her father about that special field trip to Cheff and the impression it left on her, we decided to investigate. We visited Cheff Center and cried with joy as students rode by. There was something hallowed in the beauty of the joyful, courageous riders, and their engaging, patient steeds. On the drive home from Augusta, we knew there was no pulling out of the flow now. We were hooked, and it was on to the finish line.

Cheff offered classes to become a certified instructor, so Jykla enrolled. We would need a name for our school before we registered as a not-for-profit organization.

Standing at a sink full of dirty dishes and dreaming, none of the names I came up with seemed right. As the water sloshed down the drain, I suddenly envisioned Laurie's initials LW and knew LoveWay was it! No one would know but the three of us.

Although the excitement of starting this school was great, the pain of losing Laurie was still filling our days. I was drawn to play her favorite songs and over and over, especially "Bridge over Troubled Water" and "Morning Has Broken," which were both played at her funeral service. She liked Buffy Sainte-Marie's "Moon Shot," and I sobbed uncontrollably every time I listened to it. I felt ill as the desperate agony and loss of my young, searching daughter stripped me to the bone.

I spotted a little bird outside the window that shot my mind to a precious memory of a bright-eyed little Laurie walking up to me with a little bird sitting on her shoulder. I couldn't believe it! I was afraid it might be sick. Her bird took a good look at me and flew away, so I guess it was just enjoying her company.

Looking through some schoolwork a thoughtful teacher had given us, I cried and laughed aloud. There was a paper with some pretty serious and revealing insights. Laurie was asked to draw a symbol of something she would not deviate from her whole life. She drew a cross. I was stunned!

Next came the instruction to draw something she would change if she had a year to accomplish it. She drew a family: a mother, father, son, daughter, dog, and cat—all with sad faces. A year later, they were all smiling and happy. She was then asked to draw something about trust. There it was, a man shooting an apple off a woman's head with a bow and arrow! Wow! She had that right.

Last was the question, "What are the three words you would like to be remembered by if you should die?" There in her scrawling handwriting, I read the words *love*, *peace*, and *give*. If only I could reach out, put my arms around her, and tell her what I thought of her answers. If only…

We continued with our plans, and Jykla worked hard at Cheff where studies were not a piece of cake. The books they used were on a college level on all the disabilities, the symptoms, and the care to be given for each disability encountered. Just how all of this could be transmitted to therapy on horseback was quite involved.

The selection, care, and training of these wonderful steeds were also an important part of the training. It was on the selection aspect of this Jykla and Gary would butt heads, and Jykla's excellent training would usually prove to be correct. Gary was trusting enough to let Jykla and me go to the 4-H sale with a blank check to purchase our first horses for schooling. Our excitement was at a very high level, but we knew we needed small bodies, large bodies, narrow bodies, and wide bodies to fit the many different needs of the students. We needed healthy-bodied with calm-disposition, smooth-gaited, sure-footed animals with no bad habits like biting or kicking. All this was to be observed and decided the day of the sale. Sound impossible? Well, *we* didn't think so!

Jykla studied the sale bill, checked breeds, their ages, and whether they had been ridden English or Western. She rode the horses we were most interested in and looked them over very carefully.

I sat at the rail, my stomach beginning to turn flip-flops and large rivulets of sweat trickled down my back. I had this odd sensation as I looked around that many in the crowd already knew why we were there. Word travels fast in a horse arena. I knew that from our horse show days. Mmm…So what were they thinking?

The sale began. We plunged in, and one by one, we purchased the horses we needed. It was time for ponies, and this beautiful, refined little pinto was led out to strut her stuff. Amid the oohs and aahs, I noticed the tears streaming down the face of the young lady leading her. She loved this pony named Lorrice but had outgrown her and needed to sell her to purchase a larger horse. This little pinto went English or Western, jumped, and was trained to drive. Perfect for our school!

This dear, young girl did not want her well-trained Lorrice to go to a school for students with disabilities. The bidding was fast, furious, and high. We stayed with it and did not blink an eye as the bidding went over seven hundred. There were quiet and retreating murmurs as we kept our determined eyes on the auctioneer.

The word that we were waiting for finally came— "Sold!" And we headed to the barn to retrieve our treasure. Her owner could not stop crying and gave us this wonderful little book she had made about Lorrice, telling of the way she had cared for her, how to feed her, her likes and dislikes. My heart just broke. She never came to visit Lorrice, but I wish she could have known the joy she gave so many and to see the face of the young learning disability student that won a blue ribbon in a 4-H competition. Many small hands reached to touch and curry her beautiful coat and many faces looked up from a wheelchair to receive a nuzzle from her dainty nose. Lorrice was a dependable mount that carried our proud students in parades and she did not lack for love or attention. A true treasure she was!

The work on the horses began in earnest, along with the real challenge of educating our community and schools on the wonders and benefits of horseback riding therapy for the physically and mentally challenged. We moved our new charges into the barn, already overflowing with our personal horses, to the great delight of our feed man.

Jykla worked with Gary and his wheelchair, moving around the horses with an occasional bump to get them used to such contraptions. Jykla rode with legs flopping and sometimes a little off balance to prepare them for the many new sensations they would encounter with our beginning students. My hands seemed best suited for the wheelbarrow and pitchfork. As I think I have mentioned before, some things never change.

Jykla began her quest for students. She talked to schools and organizations that served the disabled in any way. We did not even have an outside arena yet when the miracle happened—we had our first two students! Yes! So the driveway it was! What a day!

What an hour! What a success! The real thing soared higher than all our expectations.

Our first students were wheelchair-bound, and the teachers could not believe the way they responded. Tight muscles loosened, and legs relaxed from the gentle massaging received as the horses walked up and down our long wooded drive. Smiles and laughter as bright as the sunshine filled the air. In all of history and in all the stories of gallant steeds, I knew this was *the horse* at its best. This was also courage at its best—for a small child to leave a wheelchair and sit on the back of this animal, bigger than life to him, with total trust and confidence he would not be hurt. What a lesson for our life! Again, in all of history and many stories of man's gallant deeds, it is in the simple, trusting, and humble servant of the Lord that the light shines the brightest. We were all working hard for this dream of ours to grow, talking to anyone that would listen. By now, Mother was pushing for LoveWay too. Mothers are wonderful that way, getting behind their children's causes. I was touched by her understanding and concern for what we were trying to do. I also think she understood that LoveWay was becoming like a child to us. Something to live for, nurture, and watch with delight as it grew. I did wonder if her lady friends were sick of hearing about it. Maybe some of my friends were too!

"Sandy! I need to get up and get out of here!" Gary yelled.

"Just a minute, I'll be there!" I yelled back.

I knew I was giving a lot time to LoveWay but it just had to be, for now. Gary was feeling the pinch of time cut from his needs, and I was busy with all that concerned the school that I ignored any fleeting thought of a problem with that fact.

"What are you planning to do today?" I asked, helping him with his shoes.

"I'm not sure, but I need to get outside. I think I'll go for a ride. Help me in the truck, and I'll see you later."

The hand controls gave him the freedom to go, but he couldn't get out any place unless someone was there to get the wheelchair out of the truck bed. It was surprising all he could do and the trouble he could get into under the circumstances. Gary was always looking at some sort of machine, dozer, bobcat, or tractor, and I had a sneaking suspicion it was a small dozer he wanted to look at today.

I placed a plastic jug in the truck, so he could empty his leg bag in case it was a long afternoon, waved good-bye, and headed for the barn.

"We are going to have to get an arena up somewhere for classes," Jykla said, as she came in the back door with the wheelbarrow.

"I know and it better be quick," I replied, checking out Buddy in his stall. "Do you think this horse is going to make the grade?"

Smiling, Jykla answered, "Truthfully, I think he might just be our one mistake!

When the school year starts, I believe there will be quite a few classes coming, and I think we should have a good-sized arena mounting ramps for wheelchairs. I have the plans for the correct dimensions. Where do you think we should put it?"

"Gary thinks it should be in the north field, around the curve and to the left. It is all woods around the house, and the big hayfield is too valuable for feed to chop up. There would be room by the big tree in the middle of the north field, but it is a long way to take the horses. What do you think?" I asked.

"Sounds all right, but there isn't any water. They won't be drinking during class or staying there, so I guess it would be good. It would keep traffic down in your house, she laughed.

The enormous scope of our undertaking was starting to sink in; little worrisome thoughts began to peck at my brain. Gary was paying for the program, insurance, feed, and Jykla's salary. We did not pay ourselves that was never part of the plan. The school was free to all students, so the money was disappearing fast. We named the school LoveWay Projects because we envisioned the riding school as only the first project, with a camp, lodge, trails, and turning the whole one hundred acres into a retreat for those who were challenged physically and mentally.

The time had arrived to educate the community further and gain assistance to keep LoveWay growing. Fundraising was about to enter my life, and for this, I needed an education myself. Although not too poised and with no experience, I plunged in. I believed so completely in the benefits of horseback therapy, my tactics seemed to work, even over a loud beating heart, sweating, and nausea before a talk in front of an interested group. The first riding school for therapeutic horseback riding in Indiana was on its way!

A wonderful gentleman I'll call Woody arranged for help to arrive for the arena and eventually even the ramps. We hauled in loads of wood shavings and the classes began in earnest.

Now Jykla and I were into horse care, barn work, scheduling, classes, fund raising, and publicity, and last but not least, recruiting volunteers. Most beginning students required three volunteers, one on each side and one leader. A class of four required twelve volunteers. We were fortunate to have wonderful people right from the start. I found a friend for life when Agnes walked up my drive and became a volunteer.

She would take on any horse, large or small, any rider, large or small. Agnes herself was very small but only in size. Her heart for LoveWay was big. Living as close as she did, she would gladly appear when called if someone else could not make it.

It was a very busy time, and the rewards were great. It was obvious the volunteers felt the same way. They repeatedly vocalized they received more than they gave. It seems it's always that way when you give from the heart. Giving and serving God with our whole heart of love just opens our eyes to the deluge of blessings we are showered with each day.

When a tiny preschooler who hasn't talked—ever—sits on her pony and says, "Walk on," you are blessed.

When a handsome, blind, black teenager gains the courage to ride the ring alone, goes on to trail ride with his family, then downhill ski's with friends, you are blessed.

When a young lady leaves a wheelchair to sit straight on her horse and lift her face to the sun, then manages the reins herself and guides her steed alone around the arena, you are blessed.

When a young man with autism who will not let you touch him to help him up on the horse for the first time, puts his arms around his mount and hugs her after the lesson, you are blessed.

When an abused child, with wild untrusting fear in his eyes, rides, and then smiles and caresses his horse saying, "Good boy," you may cry but only because you are blessed.

These were special days.

I was ready to go the miles, whatever it took.

"I'll do it for you, Lord" was my song. I should have been singing, "We will do it, Lord. You lead the way." It would have been easier!

We did end up with a small bulldozer after one of Gary's afternoon excursions. He worked to rig it, so he could run it, but our biggest problem was getting him on. After many precarious and strained tries, we worked out a system of sorts. There was a lot of pushing and pulling from us both, but the look on his face when he sat behind all that *power* was worth it. I loved our woods, and I prayed he would leave it standing. The dozer did help us in a lot of ways, and it sure helped Gary feel useful. My main concern was the rough ride. He was beginning to have trouble with pressure sores, especially on his tailbone.

Gary also rigged our Ford tractor with levers, so he could run it, and he was cultivating our cornfield. It was an automatic, which was fittingly called our Jerk-O-Matic. The field was a long way from the house, and in order to be sure he was all right, I would run outside on the porch every once in a while and listen to hear the tractors motor.

If I didn't hear it, I would jump in the car and drive down to see if all was okay. On one such occasion, I pulled up to see him sitting quietly looking over the side of the tractor.

He motioned me to come. "Stand directly in front of the back wheel, and look down by your foot."

Doing just what he asked, "I don't see anything. What's the matter?"

"Oh, for Pete's sake, bend down and look!" He laughed. "You're always complaining you cannot find any arrowheads! There is one in front of your nose!"

I grinned. "Oh my gosh, there is…there is…I have found an arrowhead! *I found an arrowhead!* Well, sort of."

Then I noticed Gary's leg; it had fallen down against the exhaust pipe and must have been there some time. His leg was badly burned. He did not feel it and had no idea what had happened.

My glee vanished. "Gary, come up to the house now, and we will doctor your leg. It looks terrible!" From then on, we tied his legs together where they would stay put. We were always trying to heal something.

"Sandy, a lady called about a horse," said the muffled voice from the bedroom. Gary was on his stomach trying to heal a pressure sore. Just coming in from the barn, I sighed and headed for his room to hear the particulars. Someone was always calling about a horse now that we were beginning to be known. Usually, it was a very old horse that had several health problems, but the owner wanted to find a "good home."

I sat down beside the bed, and Gary began, "These people moved here from South America, and they have this young thoroughbred horse from racing stock that they brought with them. Her name is Treasure, and she is so very gentle they are sure she would do just wonderfully in our program.

I stared at Gary, not believing I was hearing right. "Of course you told her we wouldn't be interested, I hope!"

"No, I did not! I told them we would be over to see Treasure. You can ask Jykla when it would be best for her."

"Gary, you know better than to even think a young horse bred for racing would be appropriate for us now. We have no advanced students that could even be considered for that type of horse."

"I told her we would come, and we will!" was his stubborn reply.

My eyes studied the loose threads of the bedspread, and then I watched the small dust flecks dance in the sunshine streaming in the window. I followed them as they floated to the ceiling, and my eyes focused on the whaling harpoon hanging from a beam. I swallowed hard and resisted the urge to grab it and throw it into the wall.

I quietly answered, "I will speak to Jykla."

We kept the appointment. We found a particularly lovely family, a crazy Amazon parrot, and a highly nervous, young thoroughbred strained from the trip from South America.

On returning home, we began a heated discussion about Treasure. Jykla was against it, of course. Acquiring this horse went against all the instruction she was given on suitable mounts, and she felt her opinion should be upheld. That's what we were paying her for.

Gary, on the other hand, stubbornly insisted with no real logical argument. He finally said we would take the horse, and of all things, since they were moving back to South America, we ended up with Tom, the parrot. This was most definitely against my wishes.

The decision was a crushing blow to Jykla. She was expected to give the huge amount of time necessary to train Treasure for the task at hand. She did, but she was right: the horse was not for LoveWay.

Tension was growing. Gary was used to being in control and also used to having most of my attention. Although he did not have surface feeling in his legs, he did experience a lot of pain. I knew he was taking a lot of Darvon, and he was also on muscle relaxers for spasms. He also took too much to heart the advice that a doctor had given him to drink a beer once in a while for his kidneys. The doctor told him he could give him medicine to turn his urine green or medicine to turn it blue, but the best thing was to drink a beer to keep them going and cut down on infection. Well, like many things Gary did, he carried it to extremes.

God, life is getting hectic
I'm working hard for you
I want to help everybody
some days, I can't find me
Help!

Gary's High School day's

Last picture of Gary standing

Laurie and Hooligan

Laurie on her African trip

Where ever Laurie was, there also were the dogs

My dear mother and friend

New baby buff

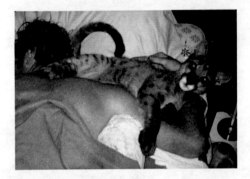

Another addition, Bsob

Gary in a bigger job than he thought

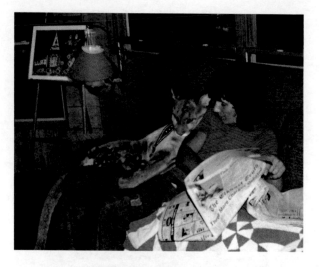

Kent and Bsob, may I read the paper please?

There is just something about that tractor

Gary and Bsob, a special love

LoveWay's beginning, in our drive way

On to desert days

Just a little warm here, don't you think?

Gary beginning to carve, atop our desert hill

My sister Jean and I having fun in Arizona

Some of Gary's carvings

Swan wagon and my great niece, Josephine

Lily Pad Walker

Swan Bowl

Cherry wood nativity set

LoveWay today

Last smooch before leaving,
Kiersten Rhinehart and friend Flirt

Some heavy work here.
Kennedy Swaenpool, and volunteer Leah Bontreger

Sure is worth it.
Kennedy, Leah, Tim Krecsmar, Instructor,
and charming Dixie

Dismount, but don't forget to run up the stirrups.
Kennedy, Leah, Tim, and Dixie

CHAPTER 7

Those who must always sit
in a chair graced with wheels,
Dream about their running free:
a miracle of being healed.
Some have never known
to move so easily;
Some have vivid memories
of how it used be.
But there is hope;
believe, even though you cry,
For on the wind with angels
someday you'll surely fly.

Our dear little home in the woods began to resemble Grand Central Station. There was constant activity and so much going on at any one moment, you could jump in anywhere, anyplace and experience something! There might be a group of "good old boys" in the bedroom with Gary reminiscing about the "good old days," while in the living room, we served thistle tea to a ladies' church group wanting to help LoveWay while praying the "good old boys" kept it down.

Jykla might be working with a horse while trying to talk with an interested client or prospective volunteer. Amid this bubbling pot was the constant ringing of the phone and the laughter of Tom, the parrot.

Tom was becoming quite a celebrity, and everyone loved him. To Gary's dismay, Tom preferred me. The fact of the matter was he did not care for men at all. After a little confrontation one day on Gary's bed, Gary decided that verbal interaction might suffice. To this day, I am able to do anything with that bird, and I do enjoy his chatter and company.

Life was lived on the run, and for me, there was not a lot of time to sit and think.

I did know that Gary was becoming addicted to all his medication and drinking too much. There was more temper and belligerence creeping into our days, especially when we were trying to heal another pressure sore. At these times, I did not think how tiresome my "just a minute!" was becoming to Gary.

Although I was waiting on him a lot—getting him dressed, sterilizing equipment for irrigating his catheter, cleaning and dressing sores—I was not encouraging him. He desperately needed some encouragement to do for himself and to and help him toward some goals of his own. Encouragement is a wonderful gift to give anyone. Our Lord and Savior have given us a whole book of encouragement, as I would begin to discover. I was also on my way to understanding my own addiction to a "do-gooder" syndrome and the faulty thinking that I as earning my way to heaven.

"Sandy! Guess what? Joe Allen called and asked us to come to Florida to see a blast off! We need a change. Let's do it!"

Our astronaut friend really put a spark in Gary's eye with that invitation. We made our plans, and there we were in steamy Florida!

"What? We can't rent a car without a credit card? But I have cash," Gary spoke politely and tried to remain calm.

We had been out of the business world for so long and had no credit cards at that time, so we did not even think about this situation arising. Our friends were somewhat upset as they expected us to be able to provide transportation for us all.

The apologies were made, the adventure continued with a spectacular nighttime close-up view of the rocket. We then were all invited to enjoy the evening meal with all the VIPs, including Walter Cronkite.

The actual blast off was unforgettable. Even more memorable was the invitation to attend another VIP event that included Alan Shepard. Gary drank too much, got into an argument with a guest, and became quite obnoxious. The only place I could drown myself was in the pool, right in front of everyone, so I opted to sit quietly and pray we would leave soon. We did.

Someone had mentioned an orange and grapefruit orchard where the owner had a private collection of exotic cats. So the next morning, we would visit a place that would have a definite bearing on our life for many years.

"They are beautiful!" Gary exclaimed.

"Yes, they are," I replied.

"They are so gentle!" Gary exclaimed.

"Yes, they are," I replied.

"I would love to have one!" Gary exclaimed.

"No, you wouldn't," I replied.

Gary then came face-to-face with a sweet, calm, Florida cougar, and they looked into each other's eyes. This lovely lady cat was going to have young, and before we left, our name was on one of the unborn.

Of course, I could believe it!

Finally back in Indiana, Gary filled Kent in on the wonderful cats we had seen.

Kent thought he would like to be a vet like his father but leaned more toward exotic animal care. Gary gleefully set it up for Kent to go down and work at the orchard/zoo with the animals and, when the cougar cub was born, bring it home. All systems go!

Back at the ranch, we were thrust into a very busy time. Classes were increasing. We began to use one of our part-bred Arabian mare, Love, in the program.

She worked well, even though she was quite young.

We needed to forge ahead on the fundraising; Jykla and I would take our slides and speeches anywhere, anytime, and we did just that.

There were always service clubs looking for a new speaker for their monthly meetings, so we were kept busy. Our enthusiasm began to bring in some donations, and the community began to hear about LoveWay!

One day, while busy cleaning Tom's cage, I happened to glance out the front window. Gary was on the dozer, busy moving some downed trees on the slope below our deck. He didn't look so busy at the moment. In fact, a closer look revealed he was buried in the mud! I thought he was at a very dangerous slant.

Running out on the deck, I yelled, "Are you okay?"

"Get a chain!" was his loud reply.

I did as I was told, struggling down the bank with a very large, long chain.

"Now what?" I said.

"Hook it around that big tree over there and then hook it on the dozer bucket. I'll try to lift the bucket and wench my way out a little at a time."

"But that will tear up the tree," I said stubbornly.

"Do you want to try to get the wheelchair down here and get me back up the hill in this mess?" he shouted sarcastically.

By now, I was covered with mud and having a hard time keeping my footing on the steep slope. I hooked the chain as he asked, he raised the bucket, and the engine roared. Nothing much happened.

His word came out like bullets, "Get some logs!"

"Logs?" I inquired.

"Get some logs!" The words almost knocked me over. "You can put them under the tracks!"

After considerable time, I hauled good-sized logs down, dug under the front of the dozer tracks, shoved them under, repositioned the chain, and got Gary a new pack of cigarettes.

Bucket up, engine revved. Violá! He moved! More logs, reposition chain, and again, he moved! He was out and on his way!

Before helping Gary off and in the wheelchair, my nose in the air, I went to the garage for the black tar and doctored the tree. The stress and danger over, we both collapsed, laughing.

These experiences were the culprit that caused so much trouble with Gary's skin, especially the tailbone area. It wasn't long until he had to stay down for a while, so his creative mind turned to trying some silver work. Walking into his bedroom, you could hardly see him under the large board on his stomach. With goggles on his eyes, he would be hammering, pounding, and soldering silver treasures. A unique candlestick emerged made of heavy silver and a deer antler found in our field and a beautiful large bracelet with a gigantic turquoise rock in the middle…for me! It was stunning, but I had to admit it would look better on "The Girl from Ipanema."

My heart was touched by the determination within Gary to do something; he was not giving up even in the predicament of confinement. Through this time of stress and sacrifice on both our parts for LoveWay, we were growing in ways I do not think we really understood. Love for one another was developing on a much deeper current that we had known before. We began to overlook many of the things about each other that had surfaced as we were thrown so closely together when Gary became so physically dependent on me.

There was an awakening that I might be taking my Ms. LoveWay role too seriously. I loved the children, horses, and the results, but I was beginning to love the accolades. I was also experiencing a desire for a church to nourish us, but Gary stated flatly that he did not.

Kent went to Florida to work with the big cats and called us with the sad news that the cougar cubs had all died from a virus transmitted by humans. However, not long after, the phone rang again, and Gary answered.

"I found your cat!" Kent's excited voice sped over the wires.

"What do you mean?" Gary replied quite astonished.

"Well, I visited an alligator farm, and there was this poor little cougar cub in a pen with other animals, and I'm bringing him home.

Gary almost jumped out of bed, even though he couldn't walk. He then began explicit instructions on how to put together a box to transport the "little cat" home on the plane.

"You can take a pet with you if it is small enough to fit in a carrier that can be held in your lap," Gary began. He told Kent just to bolt and screw the box together, so no one could get it apart and discover it wasn't just some special type of domestic cat.

Kent dutifully followed instructions, and things seemed to be going okay until just before boarding time. Kent was informed that the cat had to be placed in one of the airlines' special cardboard carriers. He took the boxes and cat into the restroom and frantically tore with his bare hands at the container he had made. I do not know how he succeeded, but he did, and he probably still has scars to prove this crazy story.

Kent flew into Indianapolis and then drove the rest of the way to Middlebury, walked in with his treasure, and deposited the ball of fur on Gary's bed. The tiny cub had a sore on his head from the pen in Florida, but he was beautiful. It was love at first sight for both of both of them! He made his home on the bed with Gary and only ventured off to carefully use the litter box. He would lay snuggled under Gary's arm or on the pillow by his head and observe his many visitors with bright and inquisitive eyes. The perimeter of the bed was his safety zone, and there he stayed. What a gift for Gary while healing yet another pressure sore and what a gift for a little cat destined for a life in a pen!

God had been so good to us, bringing helpful friends into our life and maybe the busyness was important after Laurie's death. One day, while I was mulling this all over in my mind and trying to attack the many messes scattered through the living room, the phone interrupted me. Cradling the receiver under my chin, I began to dust the table holding the phone.

"Hello. Marilyn? Goodness, I haven't heard from you in ages! Where are you living now? You've moved back here? That's great!"

The interruption from the old school chum was a welcome one.

In her amiable and gentle voice, she asked, "Could we get together? I would like you to meet my daughter, Stacy. She is wondering if there is something she could do to help with your horses."

"I'd love that," I shot back. "Anytime."

We met, and I liked Stacy right away. She was blond, very young, and very shy. Stacy's eyes were beautiful. Her face was kind but extremely susceptible to blushing. We soon realized Stacy was gift sent from heaven. She rode quite well, with much confidence, with the best hands on the reins I had ever seen.

Stacy exercised our horses, cleaned stalls, and helped in classes and all for the love of it. Stacy rode Hooligan often, and a special bond developed. Each had found a friend.

Duke, our Great Dane, loved Stacy, and he was her faithful companion on her rides with Hooligan. He appointed himself her personal protector and pledged to keep all other dogs at bay, chasing them if they even thought about barking.

One beautiful fall day, just back from a ride, Stacy remarked, "Do groundhogs usually climb trees?"

I laughed. "Not that I know of."

She giggled. "Well, one did today when Duke chased it!"

As winter approached, Stacy's dependability and wonderful follow-through attitude on projects sparked some ideas for a LoveWay fundraiser. Still holding classes outside, we longed to have an inside arena where the weather would not dictate our schedule.

We all began to dream about an endurance ride with pledges to go toward an inside arena. Moving right along with this goal in mind, the work began. We read all we could about preparing for an endurance ride, discovering that consistent workouts each day were more important than going long distances. Also to our surprise, we learned that a good rub down and deep massage each day to the horse was as important to good muscle tone as racking up miles.

The project was off and running. All of us were caught up in the enthusiasm for the adventure, and the goal ahead. Stacy began working Hooligan immediately, taking it slow and careful, checking his heart rate periodically. I would follow behind in the car clocking their time, which averaged seven miles per hour. Stacy rode flat saddle, which meant that every two seconds or so, her legs would grip Hooligan's side, and she would rise in the saddle.

It was now December, and Stacy would dress in winter attire for the workouts. As she rode, she became too warm and would begin to toss her hat, gloves, coat and sweaters into the car. This was quickly dubbed her Lady Godiva act!

There was much discussion about the length of the official ride, the starting and finishing point, and time involved.

Jykla said thoughtfully, "From all we have read, I think sixty-five miles would not be out of line, do you?"

"Do you think it should be in two days?" said Stacy, equally thoughtful.

"Aw, come on Stacy. There would be no challenge in that. You could do it in a day!" Jykla replied, grinning. "I think it is just about that from Cheff Center to here. We could check it out."

So we did, and it was just sixty-five miles. We received an okay from Cheff, and we set to mapping it out. Hooligan would have to go through a long, covered bridge, which was our only concern with route we had chosen, for fear the echo would spook him.

Stacy and Hooligan worked through the winter, and we continued to hold classes in the snow on bright sunny days. The barn was a busy place, full of fun, warmth, and air of expectancy for all that we were working toward.

The best part of it all was the response of the students, the blessed teachers and volunteers that braved the weather not knowing there would be a class or not and who gave and gave some more! It spurred us on and kept us going and dreaming!

Gary was more confined in the winter and the pain he experienced seemed greater. Again, I seemed to have my priorities confused. LoveWay was my first thought all the time. I did not understand the battle Gary was waging within himself. How could he lash out against his daughter's memorial, a memorial that giving so much to so many? He was taking far too many pain pills along with drinking beer. His attitude left a lot to be desired, but why wouldn't it? Here was a man for whom the phrase "a rolling stone gathers no moss" was written. Trying to deal with confinement, he would watch TV, talk on the phone, read a magazine, and listen to the police band radio, all at one time.

I loved him so much, but involved in my new identity with LoveWay, I missed seeing the pain in Gary's loss of his rightful headship in our marriage. He would grab for authority at times by making unreasonable demands. I would seethe inside, drop some tears, and go on, not seeing.

My longing for a church surfaced again, and I started attending a small church nearby. I tried to convince Gary to go with me but to no avail. I soon became involved with a children's Sunday school class, so I was expected to be there early.

Of course, there always seemed to be a dire emergency with Gary before I left on Sunday, and I'm sure tongues wagged about my consistent tardiness.

Asking myself many questions, I began to search for a closer relationship with God. Examining my hidden thoughts and motives definitely was not a pleasant task. Sometimes, when I felt overwhelmed, I thought, *I wonder where I would be if roles were reversed. If I was the one in the wheelchair and Gary had to take care of me! Would I be stuck away somewhere?* Then getting a grip, I'd laugh and think, *God knows best!*

God knowing best, he began to touch my life through Laura, my friend. My prayers consisted basically of cries for help with my own agenda. I was soon to learn new truths that were really never changing truths of our Lord Jesus Christ.

Answering the phone, Laura Miller's quiet but joyful voice danced in my ears. "Sandy, would you be able to go to Winsome Women's retreat at Winona Lake? It is just for the weekend."

"Oh, I would love to, but I don't know who I would get to take care of Gary and do all that is necessary for him. I really would like to. Please give me a little time, and I will see what I can do about making arrangements."

Kent's younger brother, Kaighn, volunteered, and Gary consented. I was thrilled and excited and rushed to prepare everything necessary for Kaighn and Gary to get through the weekend. I was determined not to worry and have a good time with Laura.

Finally on our way, the wonderful peace of Jesus that came from Laura enriched me like a healing balm. She talked to me of his never-ending love and the gift of the indwelling of the Holy Spirit. I didn't understand all she said, but she listened to me as I expressed my feelings about the loss of Laurie. The longing remains in me to see her and hold her.

Arriving at the retreat, we took our things to our small, sparse room and went to the dining hall. After a wonderful meal, we were treated to a fantastic speaker that lifted my heart with laughter and brought tears to my eyes. She had played Corrie Ten Boom in the movie *The Hiding Place*. Hearing about her life and Corrie's life overwhelmed me.

I have returned to "The Hiding Place" again and again to be amazed at God's goodness and mercy.

Back in the room, getting ready for bed, Laura said, "Let's pray." I began to bow my head but looked up at the movement from Laura and was startled to see her on her knees. So down I went, and that night, I learned a lot about the power of prayer.

It was a glorious weekend, though arriving home, I discovered I was properly missed. I was full of new feelings and hope for the future.

Laura presented me with a little book, *God Calling*, and it opened another window of my heart and let in more fresh, pure air. It led me to open the Bible and begin to read, even that which I did not yet truly understand.

Sandra Weatherwax

Father in heaven, Thank you for loving me
For giving me hope
Thank you for friends

CHAPTER 8

Life is like a weaving,
threads wove in and out.
Some have colors soft and quiet,
others brightly shout.
Sometimes the finest weaving
is stretched with all the wear.
The threads will snap and break,
then cry for some repair.
God, the master weaver
knows best, His work to mend.
He waits for us to place
Our weaving in His hands.

Doc Hankins, Kent's father the veterinarian, came often to visit Gary. Doc is a small wiry man though well built. Some Native American lineage is apparent in his face and, Gary thought, his demeanor. He is uncanny in his ability to diagnose.

Their friendship survived making hay together and making hay brings out the worst in anyone. When the hay is tender and it's time to be cut, the anxiety begins.

Should we cut today? Will it rain? It needs time to dry to be good, so shall we cut now or wait. Oh, it's not going to rain. Let's go for it. It will be ready by Wednesday. After all, we have a conditioner, and it will dry fast.

Wednesday: Everyone is there, the bailer is singing, and the kids are lined up along with the hay wagons to attack the heavy bales. Hey, those clouds don't look so good. *Get busy!* What? The bailer isn't bailing, right? Hey, what's this? The weatherman didn't call for rain. *It's raining!* My point is, it proves a friendship.

Doc came into Gary's bedroom, grinning and throwing his hat over the little cougar's head to play with him.

"Gary, he is cute, but he sure is going to be a big ——!"

"Yes, I believe you are right." Gary grinned back.

After Doc left, I went in to see if Gary needed anything, and he had a definite

smirk on his face.

"I've named the cat," he said.

"You have?" I asked quizzically.

"Yes, his name is BSOB!"

"BSOB. That's neat sounding. It sounds a little East Indian, very exotic. I like it. Did you come across it in a book or movie?"

"No, Doc said he was going to be a big ——! So BSOB!"

"Oh my goodness. Well, that has ruined it for me… but it *is* pretty." I sighed.

It was strange how all the ladies that came to visit, loved BSOB, and had no fear of him, even as he grew and grew. Mother would march right up and give him a swat if he wasn't behaving. BSOB was finally venturing off the bed and running through the house.

Hiding behind a corner, he would grab your feet as you walked by. Now, most men would that came to visit carried more respect (fear) for BSOB. They were very cautious of him and surely would *not* swat him. Of course, Kent was the exception. He really roughhoused with him and BSOB loved it!

I began to take BSOB for walks in the woods, even in the winter weather. He would slide and play in the snow. There was a pretty, small pond that we ice skated on, and BSOB would play on the high banks, hiding and peeking over to jump out at poor Duke and Kismet. I would run and play with all of them. I felt like I was in a Disney movie and wished Gary could be running with us. Duke never wanted to miss anything, so he would stick out the cold, even though a Great Dane doesn't have much coat for winter weather. Back in the house, Duke would practically crawl in the fireplace. He would get as near as he could, with his head on the raised hearth until the shivering stopped. On our excursions outside, BSOB would just sit and stare in disbelief at Ali Baa-Baa. BSOB never once attacked, but he sure looked long and hard. Sometimes when we were cleaning the barn, BSOB would hide in the manure spreader and peek over at us. On occasions, he would sit in the tractor seat with his attitude of "superintendent in charge of everything."

As spring came and he was getting braver, he would disappear right in front of my eyes. BSOB talked to you with a chirp that sounded like a bird. He would usually answer when you chirped at him. Well, he was getting a little craftier and didn't always call to me, so I would run through the woods chirping my head off. The exasperating part was that there were birds that sounded just like BSOB, and I was often led on a merry chase. There were a few disappointed feathered friends too!

The time was getting close for Stacy's big ride. It was scheduled for April 28, and the Junior Women's League had taken on the job of selling pledges. Stacy had worked very hard, prepared Hooligan well, and also put up with many interruptions to help us with the everyday chores at LoveWay. She also endured the stress of other trials on the ranch. One day, she was in a hurry to get home and whisked her beautiful long coat off the hall tree, started to put it on, then let out a screech!

"Sandy! What on earth happened to my coat?"

I came running and paled when I observed the almost perfect six-inch round bull's-eye hole in the seat of her coat. I knew right away who the guilty party was. BSOB! He liked to chew and nurse on thick soft material. I had seen these holes before.

"Oh, Stacy, I'm so sorry. We will buy you a new coat, whatever the cost. Please don't be upset! I'll get you any kind of coat you want, *anything!*"

Stacy looked at me incredulously but finally began to laugh, and we both howled! With relief I sighed, Stacy headed home, a little breezy in the backside.

The time was finally upon us for our big event. The day before Stacy's ride, we headed for Augusta, Michigan, with our entourage. Our car, Hooligan in the horse trailer, and a motor home filled with everyone else that would be making the sixty-five-mile trip back to Middlebury at speeds of five to ten miles per hour.

Our excited and slightly nervous group dined at the Anchor Inn on Gull Lake, along with Lida McCowin, director of Cheff Center. High spirits surely did abound around that table, with lots of horse talk and the shared love of therapy on horseback. I was proud of Jykla and her knowledge, confidence, and caring for this special utilization of horses for our wonderful and special riders.

Along with Gary, my dear mother and sister Jo was among the cheering section that night. Bob Flury, who wrote "Bob Tales" for the local paper, the Elkhart Truth, was there as the *official* observer. Mr. Flury who served on our board was himself physically handicapped. His dedication in giving LoveWay press was never topped. Stacy's younger brother came along, as did Gary's good friend, David and his wife. Jykla's boyfriend, Ralph and Lynn Ward, from Junior Women's League rounded out the party of expectant helpers.

"Let's turn in early," was the well-repeated phrase after dinner. Stacy looked grateful, as the morning bell would be at 4:00 a.m. We headed for the motel, and it seemed like I just laid my head on the pillow and it was time to get up.

At 5:30 a.m., Stacy was already busy warming up Hooligan. She was in her English saddle, wearing jeans with leather chaps.

Rubbing Hooligan's neck, I smiled. "You both look wonderful!"

Stacy smiled back, looking just a slight bit sleepy. Hooligan was prancing and seemed ready for an adventure. My heart leaped at the thought of all both had given in hours to prepare and now for the effort to ride. Tears formed in my eyes for their beauty together and for my Laurie that I missed so terribly.

"For you, Laurie," I whispered. I turned to Stacy and said, "Good luck, Stacy. We are right here with you all the way!"

We got everyone together and began the ride with much excitement! A photographer from a Grand Rapids newspaper followed us for about ten miles, jumping out of his several times to take pictures.

Stacy and Hooligan moved along smoothly, sometimes cantering, sometimes trotting, and walking in between. Hooligan had his tail up, and he was looking from side to side checking out the new territory he found himself in.

At about twelve miles, the first break was taken, with Hooligan getting a rub down and Stacy resting in the motor home. This was the pattern for most of the trip. Just before Centerville and after crossing the long, covered bridge, a needed food stop was made.

This was for Hooligan and Stacy as everyone in the motor home had been eating non-stop from the moment the journey began. It was now raining, and before Stacy would have anything, she stood in her rain slicker with a blanketed Hooligan feeding him out of a bucket. The picture is forever in my mind.

As we passed by farms and fields, horses came running up to their fence boundaries to whinny and watch us go by. Dogs came running out to bark, but Hooligan was used to the menagerie at home, and he ignored them. We were not ignored, however, on State Road 12 near White Pigeon.

An irate state trooper pulled us off the road, "What's going on? You have traffic backed up for a mile!"

I politely replied, "The state police posts have been informed of this ride." Smiling, we gave him a pledge card, and he drove off shaking his head.

Nearing home, our car was keeping abreast of Hooligan and Stacy. I rolled down the window to encourage them. My tears began to fall as I felt the courage and heart of both horse and rider. As they made their way in the rain through Bonneyville Park, less than a mile from home, a very sparse group of gathered there began to cheer. The cheering of my heart, if it could be heard, would have been thunderous.

Stacy's parents were there, filled with pride for their daughter. When Bill, Stacy's Dad, gave her congratulatory swat on the rump, he almost broke his wrist. Being able to post in the saddle for sixty-five miles takes muscles of iron.

Hooligan was up early the next day to greet his mare friends while Stacy was fairly sore and stiff. Together, they had raised over $5,000 for LoveWay. We felt it was a success.

There were other newcomers at the Weatherwax ranch, besides BSOB. Mac Makelky, Gary's dear friend from Montana, had bought us *two* buffalo! I really did not believe we were getting *two* buffalo. I thought Gary and Mac were just kidding until the horse trailer came in the drive, and *two* buffalo were put in separate stalls in the stable! Just what I needed!

"Gary! We do not have a fence to keep them in!" I said in despair.

"Don't worry. We will work something out," Gary said from his usual place in bed. They are young yet.

"Sure you will," I tried to keep control of my voice and my blood pressure.

The two young buffalo, male and female, were promptly christened, Alex and Aggie after Mac and his wife, Agnes. Alex was pretty rambunctious, so we gave him an old tire to play with. He tossed it up in the air with his horns, and it hit the ceiling of his stall over and over again. It's pretty strange to see tire tracks on a white stable ceiling.

These two buffalo would begin a series of adventures that I would unwillingly be a part of. I would also grudgingly learn to love them both. You have to understand, I do not kill spiders. I put them outside. I am a sucker!

Every time Mac arrived, even if he wasn't bringing buffalo, the pitch of excitement raised a note or two. Gary and Mac had a lot of stories to relive, and they didn't need an audience to tell them too. They just needed each other, and they would roar with laughter for hours.

Once you meet Mac, you do not forget him. Stoutly built, always wearing a beautiful Stetson hat, Western boots and carrying a voice that rattled your timbers, he was not one to get lost in the crowd.

And so the evening would begin.

"Gary! When are you coming out to hunt again? I think I'm in better shape this time and can handle it," Mac chided him.

"Are you sure? You don't look in such great shape to me!" Gary laughed.

"I've heard of buck fever," Mac howled, "but never thought you could forget you couldn't walk and jump out of the truck like you were going to run over to the edge of the canyon and take aim."

"Well, I fell but managed to pull myself to the edge of the ravine!" Gary stated proudly.

"Yeah, and as you pulled yourself along, first your pants came down, next your long underwear, then your bvd's, and there you were with your bare rear end looking for the buck!" Mac was laughing heartily.

Disturbed by all the noise, BSOB looked up from his sleep on Gary's bed, eyeing Mac's hat! He loved hats, thanks to Doc Hankins who always let him play with his when BSOB was little.

Gary smiled. "I missed him, of course. Then we both got to laughing so hard, and we didn't know how I was going to get back in the truck. Mac, you had just had a gall bladder operation and were not supposed to lift, and I was having a hard time finding something to grab on to pull myself up. We collapsed in a heap, rolling over and again laughing like girls at a slumber party!"

"Do you remember," Gary began again, "the time we were at a ranch up by Rock Springs, Montana, and we had three four-wheel drive vehicles out looking for deer? It started to snow, a real blizzard, and we couldn't see. We got separated from the others and suddenly the truck dropped. We were straddling a huge hole in the ground. We were afraid to move and it was getting dark!"

"Oh, I remember," Mac responded, chewing his cigar. "It began snowing so hard, and we knew the others would not be able to find our tracks. The front end of the truck was pointed down in the hole and we couldn't get the doors open."

"Sandy, we rolled down the windows and kept shooting off the gun," Gary said, "hoping the others would hear it."

"One things for sure, Weatherwax always had a lot of ammo." Mac grinned.

"So we rationed out our last little food, and we decided it was a good way to go…with a good friend!" Gary said thoughtfully. They both cracked up again.

I had heard the story before, but I asked again, "How did you get out?"

"Well, the other's finally heard the shots and even though twelve inches of snow had fallen in two hours, they found us. The guys hooked wenches on each side of the rear of our truck and pulled us out!" Mac said, and they were both off on another story.

This went for some time, and Mac will never know how much these visits meant to Gary. Life had become hard in many ways, but Gary's spirit to make the best of it was terrific. It was also terrific the way friends rallied and went the extra mile to see that Gary still had excitement in his life.

Again, the value of relationships was brought home to us. The love of friends and family stood far above the exasperating circumstances of life. I was beginning to see the love of God and his hands in our affairs, even when we were pulling at the bit and turning in wrong directions. God still held the reins, sometimes loosely, letting us learn but always there…waiting, waiting for us to give all direction to him and him alone. Why is it some of us find it so hard to relinquish our self-will and let the Lord do what is really the best for us?

Gary really wanted to be working. His mind was keen and ideas always flowed from him, any one of them worthwhile if they could be pursued. A gentleman came to the door one day to talk to Gary about starting a new business. After he left, Gary talked to me about what to do. Of course, we would have to come up with the money!

"What do you think, Sandy? It would mean cashing in all our remaining stock and taking a chance."

I was quiet for a while but finally responded, "With LoveWay, it's nip and tuck around here, and you want to be back working. I don't know. I guess I should leave it up to you. I'll go along with whatever you want to do."

He agonized over this decision and finally decided to go for it, which wasn't surprising. He began to prepare for going back and forth to work each day, and there was much to consider. The venture was building ambulances, and with the mechanics of this being right up his alley a new spark was visible in his brown eyes.

Later, we would regret this decision, but he forged ahead using our money to get it off the ground.

Meanwhile, everything was extremely busy for me. There were many fundraisers to become involved with, Jykla was getting married, and there were some tough times keeping everything running smoothly.

Gary and I were so much in control of LoveWay that we didn't give Jykla enough free rein, and we expected a lot in return. Becoming discouraged, she and her new husband, Ralph decided to move to Colorado, which saddened me greatly.

Fortunately, we found a new instructor in a charming lady named Dané She lived right down the road. She went to Cheff, took the course, and the transition went very smoothly.

Dané was an enthusiastic, bright, very capable, good-looking blond that always attracted attention. She was extremely gracious with volunteers and the public. We would become friends for life, experiencing some crazy times together. We had the same warped funny bone, much to Stacy's wild-eyed dismay!

Alex and Aggie were becoming quite well-known in the surrounding territory. Gary had someone secure all the fences, but they were adept at jumping over them. It became a regular habit for them to jump out and stand in the middle of the road.

Cars would come to screeching halt, find their way to the house, and the driver would ask with wide eyes, "Do you have something that looks like a buffalo?"

"Yes," I would reply apprehensively.

"What is it?" was always the next question.

"It's a buffalo!" was always the answer.

I would get a bucket of grain, go down the road, open the gate, and coax them back in. It wasn't long before this game was down to a science. Alex and Aggie jumped out, car stopped, up to the house they came to report, and I filled the pail with grain. Alex and Aggie saw me coming, jumped back in, and waited for their treat!

One poor man driving the country roads in an old green Pontiac with his Boonsberry wine hidden in a sack came in the drive. An unshaven face smiled.

"Ah, do ya haf somthin tha look lak a buffalo?" he finally said.

I sighed. "Yes."

Just then, BSOB came around the corner.

"Wha isth *that*?" he yelled.

I sighed. "A mountain lion."

He shoved his car in reverse, and I said "Dear Lord, let this be the thing that scares him into sobriety."

I headed back into the house, and I planned to set a live trap on one of our beams in the living room to catch a little lame mouse. Gary had given instructions that morning before I got him ready for work.

"Sandy, I'm getting really embarrassed at that little mouse. He runs back and forth on that beam in broad daylight, especially when we have company! Do something!"

"I can't kill him. He's lame, you know," I whined.

Gary threw up his hands and said, "Just get rid of him!"

I baited the live trap and set it in the middle of the large beam that formed the fireplace mantle.

The next morning, before dawn, I heard the trap rattling, and I got up and took the little mouse down the road, hoping it wouldn't end up in Mary Hankins' house. That day was hot, hectic, and exhausting. As we discussed the day's happenings sipping Coke, we suddenly saw a little mouse come dragging out of the woods. He went right by us, not giving us a look, and headed for the garage.

"He's lame!" Dané cried.

"He's staying!" I said, and we collapsed in laughter.

For some reason, the little mouse stayed out of sight after that.

It was Saturday afternoon, Gary was sleeping, and I decided to take a walk. I ended up in our big hay field on top of the hill. The sky was beautiful: clouds parting, the sun shining through, like you could just see into heaven.

The hay had already been made, so horses were all out grazing, along with a few cattle we had accumulated. It was a glorious sight! I sat down on the ground and just stared at the shining panorama of sky.

I kept thinking about what I had been reading in the Bible, about our Savior's return for his church, his believers, and that we would rise to meet him in the air. Oh, Lord, let me be on this hill when the trumpet sounds. Let me rise into the heavens from right here! I sat there for a long time, dreaming what it will be like to really raise up to meet Jesus in the air. I wanted to sit there gazing into the beautiful sky forever.

Oh Lord
Help me know you more
Bring Gary to know you
Help me learn to serve you
Thank You for this day

CHAPTER 9

God whispers softly, stop and listen;
we keep pushing on.
There never is a thoughtful pause
in our fast, unending song.
Laughter rings throughout this house,
seldom are there tears.
His voice still calls, come and rest,
there is not an ear that hears.
God wants to help us build our days
with His strength and peace.
Why can't we humbly turn to Him
our strivings to release.

It was early morning. There was a hint already of the seasons change that would soon be upon us. Though still warm, I was anticipating the crispness and color of autumn. Fall seemed to always penetrate my heart. It is a season of endings: the last of the vegetable gardens, flower gardens, and robins looking skyward to leave. Old lawn mowers that made it through another summer will get a long winter nap. Thinking on these things, I sighed and curled up in my favorite chair. I hoped for a few minutes of quiet before the day's race began.

I also hoped there would be no cancellations from volunteers in the classes that day because I really had a lot to do. On the other hand, it was hard to miss classes. The joy from the students fell on you like a special glittering dust that brought smiles and sweet laughter to all.

Watching riders overcome fears, growing stronger and more relaxed while riding their patient and gentle steeds was like a healing balm to me. Kyle, Doc Hankins' special needs son, rode with us. He was a blessing to us all. Through his really tough physical challenges, there was never a complaint.

Kyle's gift of "I can do it!" challenged all of us. Kyle's character enveloped all that we seemed to strive for. Kyle always had joy. He was always smiling. He had a great sense of humor and was deeply grateful. He loved my sister Josephine. One evening, they were both at my house for dinner. Jo was bemoaning the fact that she was putting on weight.

"I'm getting fat!" she stated.

Kyle looked startled. Then, with eyes sparkling, he looked lovingly at her and said, "No, you are just pleasingly plump!"

Everyone laughed and agreed.

We all began to realize that every one of our students was a special jewel, placed on earth to magnify the true worthwhile endeavors in this life. A window in my heart opened to see and hear their special message to us. Listen and see!

A gentle tap on the door interrupted my thoughts. That would be Dané. We were going to try and fill horse tanks before classes started. I reluctantly crawled out of the chair and ran to the door.

"Good morning!" I said softly.

"Good morning!" she whispered back.

"I'm not even dressed yet," I said, "but it will only take a minute!"

"I'll put the barrels in the truck and start filling them," Dané said. "I'll try to be quiet and not wake Gary."

"Okay, see you shortly," I replied.

I tiptoed to the bathroom, pulled on jeans and a T-shirt, and tried to pin up my awful, straight hair. Looking in the mirror, I realized I hadn't been giving much thought to my looks lately, and it showed. Ugh! Who has time? I grimaced, stuck out my tongue at myself, and went outside.

This chore had developed because we put fence up in the field where we had the arena and put the horses down there during the week. It was a long haul to get horses back and forth to classes. The only problem with this plan was we didn't have water available in that field, so we hauled water in barrels and used pails to dip it into the horse tanks. Even as I write this, I wonder why we didn't put some type of faucet and hose near the bottom of the barrels to save dipping! We did just pick the barrel up and dump it when it was empty enough to lift.

Riding back to the house, Dané and I talked again about the need for an inside arena. We were thrilled at the increase of students; the number would be rising over a hundred for the year. We rode in the winter unless it was extremely cold, and we had autistic students coming from South Bend. It was hard to plan around the weather, especially with those coming from a distance.

As we pulled in the drive, Dané said, "Have you seen that poor pony on the way to Bristol? It is always tied to a tree."

"Yes, I have. Shall we check it out?" I said, grinning.

Dané went over, asked the owners if they were interested in donating the pony, looked it over, and came back.

"Yep, we can have him. I think he's a great size for our little ones!" she said. "In fact, he would fit right in the back of your suburban."

By now, we had a rescued raccoon called RC that rode everywhere in my beat-up, gold suburban…with a thunderbird on the hood! He jumped in, along with the dogs, and we made the short trip to get the new pony named Breaker-Breaker.

Strangely enough, Breaker-Breaker didn't blink an eye at the crazy menagerie. We opened the door, and he jumped in the back. This little pony was a special gift, and to many small riders, he was a big blessing. Dané was a blessing too! I loved her "can do" attitude, along with her true sense of adventure and optimism. She gave my life a lift, and we did silly things like trying to smoke Swisher Sweets cigars and chew tobacco (only once). All this at *my* age! We must have looked really professional driving down the road in that old, gold suburban, the tailpipe tied up with bailing twine, and smoke pouring out of the windows from cigars we were unable to inhale! We laughed and called ourselves chick and swave…instead of chic and suave. This was Dané's invented comic relief from all that was pressing in our lives.

With Gary back to work, his life took on a new glow. His creative mind was again picking up speed. He designed an ambulance that had a sleek new look and innovative additions. There was joy in this new opportunity to be useful again. The biggest problem that loomed in his personal life was his tailbone pressure area. Long hours sitting up, even on special cushions, drove a major problem into a mega problem. Infection set in, and we knew something had to be done. This was not a good time to leave a new business with our employees, who were not new to the industry but new to us.

"Gary, we have to do something. I don't know what," I spoke emphatically.

"I know. The doctor's advice to go to the Mayo Clinic and have a muscle flap operation seems the only answer," Gary replied with deep discouragement showing in his voice. "It is not an overnight fix and not a sure thing that it will hold."

"We have done everything we can to heal it. We must give it a chance," I said, sighing.

The arrangements were made, and off to Mayo Clinic we went. There was no way I could stay for the weeks that he would be there, so after getting him settled, I made the sad and lonesome journey home.

Gary had no idea he would be there as long as he was. The infection had to be dealt with first. Then they cut each side from the hip down to just above the knee area on the back of his legs. Muscle from that area was pulled up to cover the tailbone area and cushion it. The first operation failed, and they had to do it again.

I believe there were doubts forming in Gary's mind about our decision to start another business, particularly with the unsatisfactory phone conversations he was having with employees while lying on his stomach at the Mayo Clinic. He somehow convinced the doctors that he *must* go home now. They let him leave with all the stitches in and orders *not* to sit up until he was healed and the stitches were taken out.

I went after Gary in a station wagon and put him in the back on his stomach. Back to Indiana we came. Now the problem of getting back to work! Gary immediately called a friend to help him, and he went to work designing and making a lay down wheelchair. He got a hold of some batteries from his airplane buddy Milt Hatfield and came up with a unique mode of transportation for himself. This strange apparatus was made of steel, with a narrow canvas bed just the right size for Gary to lie on his stomach. He could raise it up and down at a slant with his front body at a good angle to talk or eat at the table. The controls worked great, and it went *fast*. We outfitted it with a thick covered piece of foam, and he was ready.

I backed up the old, yellow suburban, opened the tailgate, and hauled the ramp over. Gary, with a flying start, tore up the ramp, ducking his head at the last minute to miss the car roof by approximately a half inch. Wow! Some things never change. The one disadvantage to this situation was I needed to then get in the car and drive him to work, pick him up and take him wherever he needed to go. Days were very busy!

The business was struggling financially, and Gary was getting ready to go to Vegas for a large ambulance show…in his lay down wheelchair, of course. With all the menagerie we had now acquired, plus LoveWay, there was no way I could go along to help. This show was important, as there would be many contacts made, and his ambulance needed to be seen. There had been new regulations passed, so towns across the United States would be purchasing new ambulances, and Gary had made sure his ambulance met every specification.

The decision was made to fly Gary to Vegas, where his dear friend, Mac, would meet him and help him during the show. Gary would have to sit up for the air trip, and then transfer back to his speeding bullet. I could not imagine how this could possibly work or even that the airlines could haul his speeding bullet.

Somehow, the arrangements were made, Dané said she would help me get Gary to O'Hare in Chicago. We drove an empty ambulance shell with Gary riding in his lay down wheelchair, his head right up between the bucket seats to give us directions.

To this day, I do not know how I managed to get Dané to drive, and the trip was definitely not one you would want to repeat. Gary's racetrack attitude came alive on freeways, and he began to tell Dané when to switch lanes, speed up or, should I say, hit it! I began to sweat, and Dané's knuckles began to turn white as she gripped the wheel. The big, cavernous, empty van picked up all the road noise and all our rattles, so it seemed Gary was shouting. Never have two women been any happier to see an airport than we were, at last to be telling someone good-bye.

We watched as Gary was transferred to a small wheelchair and placed on the plane. Dané and I breathed a sigh of relief, only to have another panic attack. As they were ready to put his speeding bullet in the belly of the plane, there seemed to be some problem. We were told the batteries were off limits; they could not transport them. There was some arguing, and the pilot was called. He looked them over and was amazed. He was familiar with them. He has used them in the war. They were made to be safe in airplanes. All systems go!

Dané and I waved good-bye, ran to the van, and immediately, drove uptown to Marshall Field's and Palmer House for lunch. I was not a drinker, but I did notice a beautiful, tropical pineapple drink go by on a waiter's tray and decided to have one. We both ordered, and Dané went to the ladies' room. My drink was so cold and tasted like fruit juice, so I just sipped away. When Dané came back, I was leaning my head against the vine-covered pole of our booth, sound asleep.

I rallied, and we began to talk about LoveWay, which was usually our topic of conversation. We began talking about the students and all the ideas we wanted to incorporate in the program. There was a lady sitting close by that must have been listening to us. She was all alone, and suddenly, she called to us.

"I couldn't help hearing your conversation, and I have a special grandchild. Please take this money for your program." She smiled sweetly.

We were so surprised it took a minute before Dané responded with her usual graciousness. Then she asked the lady about her grandchild and thanked her again.

After the woman left and we were gathering up our things, the waiter brought us the bill saying, "Please don't tip me. Just keep that money and put it toward your program."

Dané and I just sat there, looking at each other in disbelief.

She then howled in her usual crazy humor. "Gee, if we work this right, we could stay in Chicago for a few more days!"

We did not do that. We left there, went to the circus, and then headed home.

There was a weariness setting in with the constant flow of people through the house morning, noon, and night. Gary arrived home from Vegas with glowing reports of the reception of his ambulance. In the days that followed, we were winning bids from towns across the United States but needed capital to purchase the large van bodies to convert. It was a staggering sum, and we had already put our home on the line for this business. We also discovered many of our employees were not exactly of honest and trustworthy character. We were turned down for a loan to purchase the vans.

Mother was experiencing health problems and needed to come live with us as we had always told her she could. She was also in a wheelchair, and all this led to some serious talks. We would have to sell the house to pay off still standing loans. LoveWay would have to begin to function without Gary and me, and the board would have to become more active...*very* active! Gary had been working with a local builder to supply materials for a barn and arena in our big hay field. We would hand over this project to the board and move Mother with us to a warm climate.

Taking a good hard look at Gary, I realized he needed rest, care, and time from me that I surely had not been giving him. There was no comprehension of what the Lord had in mind for me to learn: *real* servant hood. I was serving now with the accolades of men, but that was about to change. Why is it so hard for some of us to learn that the only *true* reward is the joy we get when we are serving others in and for our Lord? I was about to receive some tough lessons, for which I will be forever grateful to my dear Father in heaven.

During this turmoil, the shock of my sister Josephine's sudden death hit us all very hard. This was the second daughter Mother had seen go before her, and her heart was broken. Jo was her firstborn and always a strong and steady support to her. My mother was a dear, strong lady herself, so she pulled herself together with God's strength and went on.

The decision was made: we would move with our menagerie and Mother to a warm, dry climate: Arizona! We left some property to LoveWay, and dear Sue Peterson, a board member, took over the reins, the building project—all of it—and forged ahead. We decided to simplify, simplify, *simplify*! We did this materially with the sale of possessions. I'm afraid we did not do so well with the menagerie…They would all go with us! The logistics of this would be mountainous.

Oh God
This change scares me
Will it be for good?… I'm afraid

CHAPTER 10

Tearing away
we are torn in two.
Hearts really looking
for all that is new.
Where is new,
in circumstance or place?
No, we will find it
in God's perfect grace.
Count it all won
to lose all the other,
And discover the joy
of one glorious treasure.

The actual physical move to Arizona was like a surreal nightmare. We had made arrangement to rent a piece of land outside Benson, Arizona. There was supposed to be electric and water already there, and we would arrive with our "home"—a fifth wheel camper—dogs, mountain lion, and parrot. Our horses would come later, and as soon as things were settled, Mother would also make the trip to her new home, a thirty-five-foot trailer beside us.

We made a strange caravan moving down the road with dogs in the car and Tom the parrot swinging back and forth in his cage. BSOB was in his house in the back of our pickup truck driven by never-say-die Kent. He was also pulling a flatbed trailer with chain link panels to put together for BSOB's pen on arrival in Arizona. The old suburban puffed along, straining with the loaded down fifth wheel behind, Gary at the wheel steering with his hand controls.

It would take another book to fully explain this trip, so I must leave it with these few words: *horrendous*, *exhausting*, and *frightening*!

Finally arriving in Benson, Arizona, in the middle of July, tired, hot, and expectant, we found a gentleman that knew where the land was we had rented over the phone. Driving down a narrow lane, my heart fell. We thought the property was ten miles out of town. It was not—it was just off the freeway.

We thought there were hookups for electric and water. There were not! I was flattened by the enormity of our situation, but we had to keep our emotions under control, and we began to search for solutions. There was an electric pole with wires running in the opposite direction up a small hill and out of sight. We followed it and came to a mobile home. With a desperate heart, I knocked on the door. Thankfully, the door opened to a couple that received us with kindness.

Yes, there was electric, but we would have to call for hookup. And yes, there was a well we would have to run pipe from. They also rented from the same man we were looking for. The next days were spent putting up

BSOB's pen and getting electric. There were some trees and shade for BSOB, but the trailer was an oven until the electric was hooked up and the air-conditioner could be used. Gary had to sleep in the bed over the fifth wheel. I got him up there by holding his legs while he crawled on his hands up the narrow steps (we called it wheel barrowing) until he reached his bed. Then he pulled himself up on the bed, exhausted.

The next two weeks were some of the most physically demanding I have ever in my life endured. I do not know if Gary felt the same, as life was surely a struggle for him ever since his accident. I thought *where* did this decision come from, and *what* are we doing *here*?

Kent had to leave for his home in Colorado—lucky man—and our work began. Gary had bonded with Harry, the man living in the mobile home over the hill. Harry wanted to help, and he surely tried but was much hindered with his advanced emphysema. If you can picture Gary in his wheelchair, Harry struggling to breathe every two steps, and myself, trying to dig a trench for waterlines in over a hundred degrees of boiling sun, you can visualize the absurdity of it all. But, praise God, a strategy of sorts evolved. We had hooked up a hose fitting on the water pump. I found if you stuck the nozzle of the hose down in the sun-baked, dry, desert soil, it dug a nice ditch for you and you could then shovel and dig out the trench for the pipe. We struggled and dug, then dug some more, and believe it or not, laughingly completed the task.

A very simple septic system was installed, and we had electric. We were living in civilization again.

We found someone to build a covered ramp from BSOB's pen up to the window of Gary's bed. A happy cat could again curl up with his beloved companion. Of course, a wire curtain had to be installed across the front of the fifth wheel opening to keep the cat from the rest of the trailer and running out the door. This was somewhat unnerving to new friends that arrived, seeing a large mountain lion *very close* and staring *down* at them. Most continued to be our friends.

The dogs made a new friend too. Blackie lived at Harry's house, but he came to visit most days. He was a large and beautiful dog with real desert smarts, I soon discovered. He also checked out what our dogs ate for dinner and began to carry his dish all the way from home and deposit it by my door. Not wanting to be rude to a guest, I always filled it with something he liked, but he left me the responsibility of returning the dish to Harry.

One morning, I took the dogs for a walk in the desert around our place and decided to sit on an old piece of wood someone left there. My heart was burdened and aching for everything left behind in Indiana. I just could not appreciate the beauty of the desert, and even though I fought it, tears forced their way out and down my cheeks. Blackie began to whine and pull on me. I thought he was showing his sympathy, and I patted his head in response. He wouldn't let up and then began to pull on me.

"Oh, all right," I said. "I'll get up and go on."

As I stood up, I heard that chilling sound of a rattle. Turning around, I saw a large rattlesnake was curled up in the shade on the other side of the wood. Quietly and slowly, I moved away, calling to the other dogs to come. I threw my arms around that beautiful big head and told him that tonight, there would be something very wonderful in his bowl.

Blackie had much ingenuity when it came to life in the desert. His favorite pastime was chasing jackrabbits. Jackrabbits can run pretty fast, but Blackie used that which was available to accomplish his goal: a Jackrabbit dinner. I heard this strange noise, a banging, as if someone was rolling a pipe around. Well, someone was. Blackie was standing on his hind feet rolling a drainage pipe over and over, pulling it toward him, and looking for all the world like a circus performer. Suddenly, out the end of the pipe ran a very dizzy jackrabbit, which didn't run fast enough to escape. Another day, I observed this resourceful dog chase another rabbit into the pipe and repeat this amazing process. I will always remember this lesson: to look around, be clever, and use what you have available.

Sadness struck when Duke, our Great Dane, began to have terrible seizures that became more and more frequent, and finally he had to be put down. We lost a dear friend and clown that we would forever miss.

We finally began to drive around some. On a trip to Arizona, we had visited St. David, just a few miles down the road. It was full of artisan wells, and there were trees and green grass. St. David was where we hoped to locate. It didn't take long to discover that along with the high grass were high prices. We were determined to keep looking.

Gary pushed on, wanting to have at least one great adventure a week. He gravitated to old mines and mountains. So off we went, sometimes many miles in one day to find his adventure. The hot, dry air was effecting the change in Gary's health that we had hoped for. He was looking better and not shaking all the time. An added bonus for me was the fact that in all the heat and hard work, I lost weight!

An interest in old mines was not my forte, but I loved mountains, so I dutifully became Gary's sidekick. One day, Gary spotted a trail up the mountain with what appeared to be tailings from an old mine at the top. Off we went, and soon, the trail became narrower and the banks on each side were steeper. Our pickup truck slid a few times, and I became just a little apprehensive.

"It will be okay," Gary said with his usual confident smile. "When we get to the top, we can turn around, and it will be easier coming down."

"I can't bear to look over the side," I said, my heart beating double time.

"Well, we sure can't turn around here!" Gary said sternly, without smiling.

The rest of the way was traveled in total silence, and when the top was reached, the silence was deafening. There before our eyes was the opening to the mine, and a fountain of shale flowing in all directions, with *no* place to turn around.

I stared at Gary in disbelief when he asked, "Do you want to get out and look inside?"

"You must be out of your mind!" I yelled. "How are we going to get out of here?"

"We will have to back down," Gary replied nonchalantly.

"You must be kidding," I yelled.

"Well, what do you want to do?" Gary asked sarcastically. "Just get out and get in the pickup bed. Sit on the tailgate and guide me left or right because I can't turn my back enough to see," he went on.

I carefully opened the door and gently slid out. As I turned to try and climb in the back, I stuck my head in the window and smiled sweetly. "If this truck starts to go over the edge, I'm jumping! Good luck!"

Inch by inch, we began the descent, my screeching… left…now right, with rocks and shale sometimes tumbling down the ravines on each side. Reaching the bottom, Gary whipped the truck around, as if it's all in a day's work, and headed for home. I hung my head out the window, wanting to soak up the hot desert wind in my face and soul. What did I see in mountains anyway?

It was almost time for the horses to arrive. It seemed the love and pride we had for our horses just couldn't be let go. I believe in my heart of hearts, I knew we should sell out horses to a good home, and I should have let Dané have Mamacita. There are times in life when love should let go. What is best for a person, animal, or relationship is many times overlooked in the name of love. If I could go back and change the happenings of the next months in our life, I surely would. But consequences go on for decisions made in our own flesh, instead of the will of God. I was about to come to the end of the trail as far as thinking I had control in my life. My true desert time was about to begin.

We found a young man from Honduras to help us build fencing for the horses. There was somewhat of a coral there, so we repaired and added fencing to get us by for a while. He spoke very little English, so sometimes it was difficult. He did understand that we were very excited that our horses were coming, and that they were very important to us.

They did arrive: Hooligan; Mamacita and her new foal; Hero, Hooligan's son; and Penny, our Quarter Horse. It took them awhile to settle down, and I was nervous because they seemed so strained and confused by the landscape.

The young man that worked on our fence helped filling horse tanks with water and with feeding, as we had a few things yet for him to do. The next few weeks were a blur, so much to do. Mother's trailer would be coming, and there would be work to get it around before my two nieces brought her to Arizona.

In all this confusion, the suburban was parked on the water hose with the keys left in it. Our young Honduras worker decided to move it and fill the horse tanks. He did not understand the hand controls, and the car lunged ahead. He ran over our horses, some who were lying down to rest. I heard him yelling and ran out to be hit with a nightmare scene.

Mamacita's foal had bones showing through her skin. Penny could not get up. Hooligan and Hero were in separate pens, so they were not hurt. I began to scream and cry. We had no phone, so I had to drive to the vet, hysterical all the way. Penny and the foal had to be put down immediately. We tried for weeks to save Mamacita, but to not avail. Her will to live was just gone.

Gary tried to comfort me, but I could not seem to get a grip on all of it. It just brought back the memories of Laurie. All the horses were such a part of her life. It seemed that I was near her when I was near them. I was sick with grief all over again. On this most evil and harsh wind, Mother's trailer arrived and then Mother herself. We had found someone else to build a small deck and ramp on the front of the trailer, as the young man ran at my first scream, never to be seen again. We went on.

Mother really needed a lot of attention. The sheer strength she had throughout her life was slowly leaving her. She wanted attention also, and I was coming face-to-face with the inevitable happening when a parent lives into old age.

My firm and stead supporter now needed me to be her firm support. I cannot explain my feelings and the difficulty I had with this. I didn't want her to be like a child. I still wanted to be the child. I did not want to really look at her and see this need. I was confused in having to bathe her, fix her food, and give her medicine, when I did all these things for my husband without a thought.

I took Tom's cage over to her house because there was more room, and she loved that. She talked to him, and he responded, to her great delight. Whenever she tried to transfer to her chair or go to the bathroom, she would say, "Oh boy, oh boy." Tom still says, "Oh boy, oh boy!" at the appropriate times.

Strange things began to happen with Gary. He wanted me to wait on him more and more, and still, he seemed very distant. It was harder to take off and go places with him. I didn't want to leave Mother alone without a phone. He began to watch soap operas and seemed as if he was more interested in the characters in the story than real people. He began to treat me very badly to the point I was in tears a lot. When I would go over to help Mother in the mornings, I could not smile, and she was hurt tremendously by my attitude.

I was not little Ms. LoveWay anymore. I had lost all of the things that filled me with earthly pride. I was in a desert place both physically and mentally. I was a servant to two people that I loved, but I was definitely not being heaped with accolades or thankfulness. I was in a strange town where no one really knew me, and there was no family near to give support.

Taking a walk, I threw myself on the desert floor. I cried and screamed at God!

"Take me, kill me, do whatever you want with me! I don't care anymore! I have nothing. I am nothing. I cannot go on!"

It was a long time before I rose to my feet. The light, but empty, feeling I felt was strangely comforting. As I quietly walked back to the trailers, there was an unexplainable release from all the pain. I was not immediately changed into perfect believer, but the Holy Spirit slowly began to do a right work in me. Step by step, day by day, life would change. I gave control to God. I gave my life to God.

I had a desire to pray more, trust more, bring my life to him to work out the many tangled threads and mend the holes. He gently began to shine his blinding light into my heart, and many sins and true motives were laid bare for me to face. I could clearly see the mountain I must climb but not the path. I was excited and ready for the journey.

There was the difficult problem with Gary. He had not shared my desert experience or my total abandonment to God. His agitation increased.

"Sandy, I must see a doctor or something!" Gary exclaimed one afternoon. "I think I am going crazy. I do not know what to do. I am hallucinating. I do not know if I am doing one thing and the other vision is a dream or if it is the other way around. I can't live like this!"

I was shocked and began to call doctors in Tucson. We finally found one that had a thought about all of Gary's symptoms. He knew of another patient that suffered with a thyroid problem and who had begun to hallucinate. Tests confirmed the doctor's suspicions, and thyroid medicine solved this terrible dilemma. Gary began to treat me with respect again! Praise God!

Still very homesick and feeling the need of some women friends, I noticed a small announcement in the paper for a meeting of a writers' group. Deciding to give it a try, I made a note to attend. I am glad I did, as I made friends that I have to this day: Dear Dorothy, with her encouraging outlook and her love of music and art; and Sylvia, with her poet's heart and beautiful watercolor expressions. They were refreshing water to me in my servant state of life in the desert. But my real refreshment began to come from God's word and his love. My thirst for him increased as the days went by.

The old suburban gave up the ghost, and we just had the truck. When we headed for the mountains or festivals with Gary driving, Mom was in the seat beside him, and both wheelchairs along with me in the pickup bed. Luckily, it doesn't rain too often in Arizona. We really did have some good times and enjoyed some wonderful views.

On Mother's ninetieth birthday, we had some friends come by for cake. We reordered her telling about her life and all the changes she had seen. She grew up with a horse and buggy as a child and young lady, watched TV become commonplace, and saw the first moon landing. Ninety years in the United States brought a whirlwind of changes in how lives were lived. I know Mom thought that not all were good.

Mother was becoming weaker and weaker, and there were short visits to the hospital. Finally, she could go no longer. She had told me she saw Jesus standing at the foot of her bed. Now in the hospital, her veins collapsed, and she was asking to die.

"Please let her go," I pleaded with the doctors as they kept trying to find a vein in her foot.

"We cannot do that without the rest of the family's authorization!" they stated coldly.

I ran to the phone and called my brother in Indiana and asked someone to talk to him, but they ignored me. While I was gone, they put the IV in her foot. She was in so much pain.

"Oh dear God, please take her to you," I cried. And in a few days, he did.

Oh Precious Savior
Be with us now
My heart is longing for you to
envelop us in your peace
I love you
I'm crying
I need you
I love you

CHAPTER 11

Desert days, simply framed
in transparent, pure, hot light
Bring shadows flowing deep
into the starry night.
Hot winds dry sorrow tears,
open eyes begin to see
Striking beauty missed before
is suddenly set free.
God's breathless beauty shines;
it burns away the chaff.
His grace the heavy weights release,
His love becomes my staff.

Days began to wear new colors, as if I donned new wide-horizon glasses that allowed me to look at life with clear and simple thankfulness. Joy came in small, simple moments of a cool, refreshing glass of water in the desert heat and hot breakfast coffee with a friend.

The pure lines of the desert, distant mountain ranges, and sky held me transfixed and quiet in the awesome wonder of God's majesty.

Knowing I did not want to be ruled by the world anymore, I began to hunger for more of God's word. It was there I found that my real battle would be with myself. Christ's own words came alive and their truth penetrated my heart.

> Then said Jesus unto his disciples, "If any man will come after me, let him deny himself, take up his cross and follow me. For whosoever will save his life, shall lose it; and whosoever will lose his life for my sake, shall find it. For what is a man profited, if he shall gain the whole world and lose his own soul? Or what shall a man give in exchange for his soul?"
>
> (Mathew 16:24–26, KJV)

Wow! I began to think in terms of eternity. The realization that life here could be marked by a parenthesis, but life in eternity was something else. A life unexplainable real forever more!

The search and growth began. Searching my heart for those things I wanted to be rid of, which brought me to my knees many days, asking for forgiveness, I searched the scriptures for the sure, the true path to God.

I ran right into the smiling face of Jesus, the way—the only way!

"Jesus, help me," is the shortest prayer I said and even today that holds true. I think I have prayed it thousands of times. It rises from me so many times a day. It is almost constant, and so is *he*, then follows,

"Thank you, Jesus!" I'm sure there are smiles in heaven at my stumbles, but isn't forgiveness wonderful?

The wonderful realization of Jesus dying that horrible death on the cross for me—for *me*—that he was the sacrifice, the pure sinless lamb of God, and because of that, my sins were forgiven no matter how small or big I thought they were.

I always wanted to rush over the sacrifice of animals in the Old Testament of the Bible. Loving animals, I couldn't stand to think of it or read it. Now as I read the words in the Bible about Jesus, the pure sinless Son of God, beaten, spit upon, nailed to a cross and mocked, for me and for you…the terrible and beautiful truth of sacrifice engulfed me. It was all leading to this one moment, the complete, perfect sacrifice for mankind. I cried.

Having received a small, unexpected check, we finally bought a piece of property in the country between St. David and Benson. It was pretty bare but did boast a hill, which always attracted Gary. Hopeful for an artisan water flow, and after finding one; we immediately added a small pond and planted some almond trees.

My Midwestern roots really thirsted for some trees, and I guess Gary's must have also. He spotted two huge palm trees in Tucson that needed to be moved. I never figured out how, but he managed to find someone to move them to our property. He had them placed on a small rise to the side of and above our trailer. Then we got help to put in railroad tie steps up to them. With nothing else up there, it looked like it might be a place of sacrifice following Old Testament days. We took a lot kidding about that!

The nearest thing to sacrifice under those palms was Gal, my dog, and me. One evening, we were sitting outside enjoying the last colors in a fabulous sunset.

"I'm really tired. I think I'll go inside and lay down, if that's okay." Gary sighed.

"Sure," I replied.

I got Gary in the hospital bed that just fit in the small tip out of the trailer, set up his water glass, hooked up the leg bag, and then the loud snorting began!

Immediately, the dogs, Blackie and Gal, started barking furiously but did not leave their spot on our little overhang porch.

Gary said, "You better check it out! It might be javelina. Take my pistol in case you need it!"

I just stood there, looking at him. "But won't they just go away?"

"The dogs are going crazy, go ahead. It will be alright," he responded.

Gingerly picking up the gun and a flashlight, I slid slowly out the door. The noise was coming from the backside of our majestic palm trees, so I crept up the steps.

I turned and whispered to Gal and Blackie, "Come on, guys, I need you!" They stared at me refusing to move. "Well, thanks!" I muttered.

I turned and started up again. My flashlight started to blink, and I shook it, but it only flickered a few times and then went out. The moon was coming up so bright, I didn't think I needed it anyway.

The snorting started again and, I looked up to see the biggest javelina I had ever seen was silhouetted above me in the moonlight. I started shaking, and I realized he had his harem with him and all the ladies seemed to be in turmoil. There might have been a rival mixed in somewhere. Anyway, he did not appreciate my presence, so he charged.

Off the porch came the dogs, Gal in the lead, Mr. Javelina turned to charge her. I fired the gun, but it did nothing but make him *very mad*, so I turned and ran with Gal and Blackie at my heels. We ran into the trailer, slamming the sliding door behind us.

Panting, I yelled, "That gun did nothing!"

Gary became thoughtful, then said, "Well, ah…I think there is just bird shot in it for snakes, it probably didn't even phase your javelina. What was that you were saying as you ran down the hill? I could hear you from inside."

"If you heard it, then I don't have to repeat it!" I replied fuming. "*That* was the biggest javelina I have ever seen," and I showed him, raising my hand up past my knees to show how high he stood.

"Now, Sandy," Gary said, laughing, "you were looking up at him, and at night, he seemed bigger."

"No," I insisted. "He *was* that big!"

"Well, whatever," he snickered.

They finally left, and Gal and Blackie ventured outside again.

About a week later, we were invited to a cookout on some property quite a distance behind us. There was a gentleman there that evening talking about a sighting of the largest javelina he had ever seen.

He raised his hand up past his knee. "It stood about *that* high!"

Everyone grinned, thinking he was exaggerating. I glared at Gary, waiting for his reply. He mumbled something about seeing one at our house—ha!

I took this gentleman aside and said in a low and convincing voice, "I believe you!"

These were the days of hard work in the sun, making sure everything was irrigated properly. Gary was restless to be doing something and working with his hands.

"I would like to do some carving," he announced. "Let's try to find some wood I can work with."

We found some large pieces of mesquite, cottonwood, and some oak. Sitting in his wheelchair on our little porch, bent over, brandishing a chainsaw, he began shaping his first piece. Then he began his handwork, and after many days, it became his first swan, hollowed out between the wings for flowers or fruit. He wanted to give it to someone special, so he sent it back to Indiana to my niece, Heidi.

As time went on, we purchased some tools, and his work became more refined. I felt the joy he was experiencing working with wood. He would work each day on the porch until it became too hot, forced to retreat to the air-conditioning. We attended a few art festivals, and he was commissioned to do a large seagull—yes, in the desert—with its wings outstretched, which turned out beautifully.

No telling of time in Arizona would be complete without the remembrance of my dear sister Jean. She decided to take a sabbatical from marriage and take it in Arizona. She started West with a small car pulling a small trailer to live in but couldn't make it over the mountains. She then traded the small trailer for a small hauling trailer and roof carrier. Shoving what was left over in her car, she headed for Benson, Arizona.

Jeanie's arrival was pretty spectacular! As she turned on the highway leading to our home, the men working on the telephone lines were amused as ladies unmentionables began flying through the air. Looking in the rearview mirror, she noticed some familiar items sailing about, the large suitcase on the roof carrier had popped open and its contents were blowing merrily along the road. She stopped and spent some time picking them up, she never mentioned if the telephone workers helped or not.

Turning in our drive, she eyed the hill and then decided to give it a whirl. Jean made it, almost to the top, but not quite. Gary was gone with a friend, so we hugged and talked until she decided she wanted to go look for a place in Tombstone before it got too late. We unpacked a few things to store for her, and she tried to back down the hill. The trailer just wouldn't keep straight in the sand, so we decided to unhook it and walk it down. Then she would back her car down, and we would hook it up again.

"Just hang on right there," she told me.

I hung on for dear life, as she unhooked the tongue from the ball, and we started down the hill. It went faster and faster. We couldn't slow it down, and we began to run. I was running as fast as I could, and I couldn't hang on any longer. As I let go, I was amazed to see she still had a hold on it and was running like I could not believe. All of a sudden, her hands flew up and the little trailer sailed the rest of the way to the bottom of the hill and flipped over on its top, wheels spinning. We collapsed on the ground in hysterical laughter.

After regaining our strength and still giggling, we managed to get the trailer upright again, which was no easy feat. As Jean drove off, I wondered if every day with Jeanie was going to be this exciting.

I walked back into the trailer, thinking about my expectations with this unexpected time to spend with Jean. She was thirteen when I was born, and there were two older sisters, Maxine and Josephine, and our brother Robert, who was sixteen.

Mother was in her late forties when I was born, and as I grew up, it was hard to relate to my older siblings as brothers and sisters. They were away from home by the time I was fully aware I wasn't an only child. Mother came from a generation that didn't talk much about the changes in a young girl's life as she matures and my sister Jean became a surrogate in that department.

She told me in the most beautiful way what it meant to become a woman and took me shopping to buy my first grown-up underwear. I guess Mother hadn't noticed.

I hoped this would be a time to bond together again. We had drifted apart as happens so many times in families. There had been misunderstandings, and I prayed for those things to be resolved. Too much friction in families is caused by thoughts that are completely off base, not even near the real truth. On top of that, we expect everyone to behave perfectly…except ourselves. Of course, the final truth in the matter is, Jesus taught us to forgive.

> For if ye forgive men their trespasses, your heavenly Father will also forgive you: But if ye forgive not men their trespasses, neither will your Father forgive your trespasses.
>
> (Matthew 6:14–15, KJV)

> And be ye kind one to another, tender-hearted, forgiving one another, even as God for Christ's sake hath forgiven you.
>
> (Ephesians 4:32, KJV)

I read these verses with much interest; there were no exceptions listed!

After Jean became settled, we wanted to do something together. So a watercolor painting class was decided on. Jean already was an accomplished artist in oils, and I always wanted to try watercolor. Our teacher was a retired military officer, and he ran his class in the fashion he knew. Sit up straight, be quiet, stroke here, brush there. His work was nice, but it didn't seem to fit our idea of watercolors. We forged ahead anyway but soon found ourselves getting bored, which led to silly. He lectured a lot, so during one of these sessions, Jean drew a funny little boat and passed it to me. I tried to stifle a giggle and drew some funny little people in the boat and returned it. This went on for a few minutes, and the giggles got louder.

Well, to make a long story very short, we were properly chastised; and when Jean accidentally spilled her water on one his painting, we felt it was time to move on.

Running around together, we did have fun, and many old strains were loosened with an almost childish freedom of camaraderie. We settled in for some serious discussions too. One of Jean's dear girlfriends came to visit, and Gary took us across the border into old Mexico.

Jean had always fought with her weight, and while there, she bought this gargantuan poncho and put it on. We were walking down the street and a couple of boys grinned at her.

As they passed us, they said, "Hubba hubba."

We just collapsed laughing. It was a fun day I won't forget. We shopped and laughed and laughed some more. Jean's sense of humor and fast wit was more apparent than ever before. Talking with Jean, I learned we shared an intense feeling for the beauty of nature and we enjoyed many of the same things. It was a blessing.

Thinking again of our conversations about the alienations in families, especially between siblings, I wondered how we would feel when stood before Jesus to account for our life. I cannot picture myself saying, "But, *she* did this and *he* did that!" I *can* see myself on my knees at his feet asking for forgiveness.

The most wonderful moment in your life comes when you ask Jesus to come into your heart and you ask forgiveness for your sins. You are forgiven and the love of God will give you the grace to forgive others. Praise God!

There were many wonderful people we came to know and love in Arizona, but the stories of our friendships with them would take yet another book. It would suffice to say most were hearty individualists that stretched our minds in new ways.

Although I appreciated the desert, the life and culture there, I was still aching for home. Gary was trying particularly hard to please me on my birthday, as he knew I was getting restless about going back to Indiana. We went up in the mountains with just your basic camping gear: sleeping bag, water, food, utensils, matches, and high spirits.

After driving around and enjoying the scenery for the day, we picked a secluded spot to spend the night. Secluded was the plus side; the minus was it was on the other side of a fairly steep embankment and small stream.

"We can make it," Gary said excitedly. "After all, it's your birthday!"

"Not with the truck," I quietly responded.

"Oh no," he said. "You'll have to carry all the stuff over, and I'll get in my wheelchair. You can push me through *that* little stream."

"Happy birthday!" I muttered to myself.

After lugging the cooler, the utensils, the sleeping bag, and the water jugs, I found I had left my high spirits along with Gary on the other side. I struggled back, got behind his chair, and we began the descent down the bank. I couldn't help but think what the trip back was going to be like.

We made it surprisingly easy, and I began to straighten up our little campsite.

Gary crawled out his chair and built a fire with mesquite wood we had rolled in our sleeping bag. When the coals were just right, he gently laid our steaks on the glowing bed of coals and tended them until they were done.

Handing me a streak, he grinned. "Happy Birthday!"

I grinned back. "Thank you."

One bite told me this was the best steak I ever had in my life!

"I love you," I said softly.

"I love you," came the reply from the fantastic chef on his stomach.

After dinner, I cleaned up the mess, and we just sat enjoying the quiet and the sprinkling of stars blinking through the trees above us. Finally, I rolled out the sleeping bag, and we managed with some difficulty to both get in the one sleeping bag.

Getting comfortable as last, we felt a few raindrops hit us in the face.

"Oh no!" I cried. "It can't rain."

"Let's stick it out. It may not rain hard," was Gary's optimistic reply.

It did not rain hard. We slept soundly and were awakened in the early morning by several deer passing right by our heads. A terrific birthday!

Oh Father in heaven
Thank you for your world
Thank you for this moment...
Bless Gary

CHAPTER 12

Old familiar scenes
danced within our heads,
Like old favorite books
calling to be reread.
Hearts that never left
the vestiges of home
Now ached to know again
paths where we had roamed.
The tug became a pull
stronger every day;
I felt the future turn,
we would never stay.

Jean had returned home, and I missed the time I had grabbed from other duties to be with her. Sitting on the steps under the palms, I was amazed at all the birds that flew in and nested there. The chattering in the early morning coolness was comforting, and I thought of my sister Maxine. I wish I could have known her better too. Maxine died at the age of forty-seven, a time when I was busy about my husband's bidding. There were some real regrets I felt about that sister relationship also. I thought how wonderful it would be if all of us could be together chattering away like the happy birds above my head.

I thanked God for the gift of communication that Gary's disability had provided in our marriage. Our forced togetherness became a platform to discuss just about everything. We did not agree on all things, but time spent in long talks cemented our feelings for one another. In this husband-and-wife relationship, we uncovered some deep streams of shared loves and thoughts.

Sorting through a box of pictures that had just surfaced, I was studying a picture of Gary before his accident. Now looking up at his smiling face, I was stunned.

The face in the picture wore hard, piercing eyes, a stubborn set jaw, and no sign of gentleness. The face I observed across from me quietly reading was yielding and had brown eyes soft with compassion.

Thankfulness flooded over me for our trials, along with a new acceptance of God's ways in our life. Relating my thought to Gary, I hoped he would understand.

Gary's immediate reply confirmed he did totally.

"I would like to be able to walk again more than anything in the world, but I wouldn't want to walk and be the man I was before the accident," he said softly.

Instant tears fell down my face, and I managed to squeak out a muffled, "I know."

Tom broke the following silence with a tirade of loud chatter, and we both laughed.

"You crazy old bird," I said, getting him a treat from the counter. "You are always in the middle of everything."

Gary grinned. "Remember the time his cage caught on fire?"

"Do I? I'll never forget it!" I replied, and we were off, pulling up another hysterical story.

The tale began when a brave veterinarian came to give BSOB a shot. There was light snow on the ground, and BSOB was out on the deck having a high old time playing on a wooden railing. We had given him a mild sedative, but it seemed to have put him in a roaring, silly mood instead of relaxing him. News traveled fast in our little neighborhood, and the Tackett family showed up to see a veterinarian get mauled. They were all lined up on the inside in front of the windows facing the deck. Behind them, the fireplace was spitting and crackling merrily. Tom was in front of the fire, and he was snuggled against his cage as close as he could get to soak up the warmth.

BSOB would not calm down. He raced up and down the deck and out maneuvered the poor vet at every turn. When the disheveled vet slipped on the wet snow and landed flat on the deck himself, I thought I'd better go out and help. BSOB might think it was part of the game and jump on top of him. I could not contain him either. He was not mean, just having a jolly good time. Gary came out on the deck in his wheelchair; that was to no avail. BSOB bounded around him like there were springs on his feet.

I turned to glance inside, and there behind the row of staring eyes were flames licking up the sides of Tom's cage. I yelled and pointed for everyone to look behind them. They stood transfixed, as if now I was putting on a show. I pointed and yelled again. Still no response. So I ran down the deck, tore open the porch door, ran to the living room door, pushed it open, ran to the cage, pulled Tom out, ran for water, and dumped it on the cage. Faces and eyes had finally turned, staring in disbelief as I clutched the counter, panting.

We tried a different strategy with BSOB. Gary got into bed, and we let BSOB in. When he jumped on the bed to love up Gary, a very quick vet gave him the shot, and it was done.

Telling this story again opened the moment for me to bring up my concern that BSOB couldn't get in with Gary now. Gary went down in his pen a lot, but it wasn't the same. He had protection from the sun and his own little pond, but I was sure he was not happy.

"I know." Gary sighed. "We will have to work on that."

While in Arizona, we spent a lot of time investigating the intriguing places around us we spotted on the map. Most were an all-day trip, as you know if you have spent time in Arizona. Gary's curiosity and ability to make friends anywhere led us into many adventures. I tried hard to be enthusiastic for him, but my homesickness was beginning to be an ache I couldn't shed.

One day, I went into the post office by a small shopping center, and sitting in the van, I opened a letter from home. I read it quickly, then started screaming, yelling, laughing, and throwing my arms in the air. I ignored all the stared, whipped my van around, and headed home.

Running into the trailer, I waved the letter and yelled at a startled husband, "There's going to be a baby in the family again—a baby! Tina is going to have a baby!"

"Well, whadda ya know!" came the response.

I was so excited that my niece Christina was going to be a mother. I felt our family needed a baby; it truly did! I was just plain ecstatic, and of course, now more homesick than ever.

I tried to concentrate on the reason we came here in the first place, Gary's health. Gary was still carving, and he had some success at small art shows. The one problem that loomed large over everything was finances. It took many hours to create his sculptures, and the money didn't go far enough to cover all our expenses. Gary really wanted to work at a regular job again. He was always sketching his ideas and inventions and dreaming of ways to get them in production. He truly was a production genius. We both wondered if we went back to Indiana, if a niche would open up for him to work again.

We sat on our little front porch and watched a glorious sunset performance. The horizon was filled with intense red and gold waves, like an ever-moving ocean in the sky. I thought I could stare at it forever. God, this planet you gave us, how wondrous it is! How filled with your divine thoughts: the intricacies of each plant, animal, human being, and even of my eyes…to behold your beauties.

Oh God, why does man fight against your perfect truth and order? We ravage the beauty you gave us in nature and in spirit. Forgive us.

The sunset dropped away, and soon in its place, the heavens filled with masses of sparkling stars. The desert air became cooler, and not wanting to leave the display of twinkling lights, I ran in the trailer for jackets. Gary brought some wood on his lap, and bending over in the wheelchair, he filled our fire ring with cheery warmth.

"Looking at the stars on a night like this makes me realize how big God is and how small I am," I offered.

"I know what you mean," Gary replied.

We sat in silence. Sometimes catching sight of a shooting star, we cried, "*Oh look!*"

The fire became glowing embers, and I noticed Gary beginning to shake.

"I think it's time to turn in, don't you?" I asked.

"Yes, I'm ready. The coyotes are beginning to yip. I think we must have coyote condos behind us. They sound so close, and there are so many."

"I'll take a walk tomorrow morning and check it out." I laughed.

The next morning, Blackie, Gal, and I did that very thing. I think Gary was right. We did see a lot of what appeared to be coyote dens along the dry riverbed. They were death on cats, especially in the desert where trees were few to run up and escape. Sometimes, they would send a female in heat to coax out a dog, and then a pack of them would show up to attack the dog.

One morning at daybreak, I fixed a cup of coffee and slipped outside quietly to survey the desert landscape.

What I observed was an amazing occurrence. First, I spotted a lone coyote working his way toward our hill. He was moving stealthily looking first one way and then the other. I immediately scanned the surrounding area for Gal and Blackie. Then I saw Gal, who was a small dog, head straight for the coyote in a nonchalant manner, as if she didn't see him. All of a sudden, the coyote bolted right for Gal. She turned and ran, leading him toward a fence line where Blackie was hiding, and out he burst. Gal turned, and with Blackie, they chased that coyote for all they were worth. He was running for all he was worth, and they were on his tail. I don't know how far they went. I lost sight of them. When they returned, they were panting, their tails were wagging, and they had big doggy smiles on their faces. I figured the coyote was still running. I guess Blackie learned a lesson very well: two could play the game. I wouldn't believe this tale, but I saw it!

Gary was beginning to think carefully about going back to Indiana too. One day, when we were talking about it, he said, "Let's drive down to Bisbee today." He really loved that town, and the copper mine there was the beautiful Bisbee blue turquoise that was found in it. He was also fond of the Copper Queen Hotel, and truthfully, I would have liked to erase a few memories of moments there.

Our first visit we had worked together to get him up the very steep and long row of steps to the hotel with his chair precariously balanced, and me hanging on for dear life. I could hardly enjoy my lunch there, thinking about going back down.

But the very worst time came about while entertaining visiting friends from Indiana; at least, they *were* friends before this story I am about to tell. We were going to Bisbee, show them the town, have dinner, and spend the night at the Copper Queen. We made it there just fine, but I wanted to check on our rooms, as we had not really seen them.

"Gary, you take them around the town. I'll check our rooms and wait for you at one of the outside tables," I said graciously.

"That sounds just fine. We will see you in a short while," Gary said, and he grinned and waved out the van window.

Going inside, I took a quick survey of our rooms, checked with the dining hall, and bought a Coke to drink at one of the outside tables. I was sure it wouldn't be too long before the red van would be flying around the corner, and we would be enjoying an evening with our friends.

I met some people traveling from Michigan. In fact, they lived close to our friends, the Niblocks, who were riding around with Gary. After a good long conversation with them, I began to get a little nervous. I kept looking at my watch; they really should have been back by now.

Time ticked by, the evening was fleeing, and still no Gary. Where on earth could they be? I walked around the Copper Queen, went down the street looking both ways straining to see a red van headed my way. My disgust began to turn to worry. Maybe I should check with the police or hospital or *something*!

I went back up the steps to the hotel, and as I walked in the door, I heard my name being paged. "You have a phone call," the gentleman said. Picking up the phone, I fearfully said, "Hello?"

"Sandy, your husband is crazy. He is just crazy. I cannot believe him. He is crazy." And then there was a tirade of words I could not understand. I finally pieced together that Gary took them up a steep street above the hotel, and there was nowhere to turn around. While Gary was trying to turn, the van slid over the edge of the mountainside and was hanging there by one wheel. Our friends, Chet and Mary Lou, bailed out. Gary was still in the driver's seat. Someone had come to help, and everyone was trying to hold the van to keep it from going down the slope. Mary Lou took their suitcases out, which really started Gary laughing. The police were called, and Mary Lou went to a house to call me, screaming and telling me that Gary was nuts because he just sat there laughing. Through all of this, I hadn't uttered a word. I didn't have a chance.

Mary Lou slammed the receiver down, and I just stood there, staring at the happy people walking by.

Why? I asked God. Why?

With ropes, chains, and people pushing, they finally got the van righted around and started back down the curvy and steep road. That was not the end. We had failed to fill the van with gas before we left, and he ran out, which locked up the steering on the way down. I have no idea how they made it to the bottom, but they got gas and *finally* made it to the Copper Queen.

Gary was still shaking from laughter. Mary Lou was not speaking except to scream about my crazy husband. Dinner was strained, and the food was not good as the dining hall was about to close. We finally made it to our rooms, and I helped Gary get comfortable, taking care of all his necessities. I fell into bed hoping for the escape of sleep.

I felt the bed shaking and switched on the light. There was my husband, not even trying to control himself, shaking all over from laughter.

"Stop it," I said. "*Are* you crazy or something?"

"You had to be there." Gary laughed. "There I was, ready to go over, and Mary Lou is screaming about her suitcases," and he just broke up again.

I rolled over, pulled the covers over my ears, and tried to go to sleep. Periodically all night, I felt the bed shaking, and I sighed. Some things just never change.

Well, this trip to Bisbee was not so eventful. In fact, it was sweet. Gary bought a few small pieces of Bisbee Blue to make a ring for me. We talked again about going home to Indiana. I felt it really might happen.

I wanted to badly to be in God's will. I felt remorse for so many things I had done. Where do you really want us Lord?

> For all have sinned and come short of the glory of God. Being justified freely by his grace through the redemption that is in Christ Jesus.
>
> (Romans 3:23–24, KJV)

Grace…What a beautiful word! I read it over and over. Looking it up in my dictionary, I smiled as I read two of the definitions: "favor or service freely rendered; the unmerited, but freely given love and favor of God toward man."

Dear Jesus
I love you
Guide us
Thank You for loving us
Thank you for salvation, eternity, and *Grace*.

CHAPTER 13

A dusty country road
leads us to our land;
Tall un-mowed grasses
reach to touch my hand.
The sweet breeze of summer
and green beneath my feet
Bring heavy scented air,
wild raspberries, drippy sweet.
Peace invaded our being;
smiles burst upon our face.
Joyfulness will overflow
and hold us in this place.

We decided to go back to Indiana and park our trailer on a hill we had not sold. There were many wonderful and interesting people in Benson that we would miss, but Gary wanted to *do* something…to work again. He had discussed a project he believed in with someone in Elkhart and planned to pursue it when we got settled.

Kent had taken Hooligan to Colorado for a while, so we had BSOB, Gal, Blackie, Tom the parrot, two cats—Pia and Snoopy—to move along with us. Some brave friends from Benson decided to help us, so when our land sold, we headed for home.

This trip was not a piece of cake either, and this time, I was behind the wheel of Old Blue, our truck. I had BSOB in the truck bed and pulled a flatbed behind with his cage. Gary drove the van with the dogs, cats, and Tom. Our friends pulled our little house trailer. We were not far down the road when we noticed Gary was weaving around and finally pulled off the road. I called on the CB.

"What's going on? Are you all right?"

"Yes, I'm fine, but Blackie is in my lap. I think he has to go to the bathroom!"

"Oh," I said, relieved. "I'll get him out."

That is sort of how the trip went. But as we hit southern Indiana and the green earth smell blew in my window, I was revived. Getting close to Nappanee, we could smell the spearmint fields, and Gary was exuberant.

We made sure there was a well and electric before we arrived. Gary had flown home after our desert land was sold, and his dear friend Dave drove him around and made all the arrangements. On this quick trip, he was also privileged to be the first of us to see my niece Tina's new baby girl, Josephine.

Thank you, God, thank you, God, was all I could think.

We got BSOB's house set up, and he even seemed glad to be back. Poor Blackie was used to the wide-open spaces and seemed confused with the tall grass and the trees in the woods. He was not in his element, and I felt sorry for him. The cats were happy and loved being outside without fear of the coyotes. I began picking the wild raspberries, eating more than I put in my basket.

We hired an Amish crew to put an addition on our trailer. It was an interesting room built on posts, like a deck that was enclosed. It was great as we didn't feel so confined. And wonder of wonders, I finally had a washer and dryer! I lived the years in Arizona without one and spent many hours in the Laundromat.

One of the young Amish men that worked on this project reached out in a humbling act of kindness. He came to me with his weekly hours and asked if I would cut his pay. I was stunned. Cut his pay?

He was so shy and said in a quiet, soft voice, "I can get up and go off to work so easily, and Gary cannot. I just do not feel it is right, *not* to take less."

With tears wanting to burst forth, I held my composure and thanked that special young man. *Oh God*, I thought, *I thank you. I have seen you in so many different people. You are everywhere! Why do we think in terms of this church or that church? If we love you, accept Jesus Christ, and are obedient to your word, we are your church—all of us—your church. How glorious it will be when all who are yours, from every country and every tribe are together singing and worshipping you in heaven. I can hardly wait!*

It was the weekend, and I went out in the early morning to feed BSOB. I hadn't heard him chirp at me, and when I opened the gate, I saw him lying in front of his house, not moving. I ran over and then screamed as I realized he was dead. Crying, I ran in to Gary. He pulled out of his sleep to get up, not believing what I was telling him. We had not known anything was wrong at all.

The wind was blowing softly as we buried him on the crest of the hill, overlooking fields across the way. I hope all those who came to know BSOB and love him are blessed with new appreciative eyes of God's creation. For him to live in captivity was worth it, especially when you hear a young man say he could never shoot one of these animals after knowing BSOB. In the West, they actually catch and cage these animals, then let them out near a hunter paying for the privilege of shooting it. Likewise, the inhumane treatment and suffering we subject on innocent animals, parallels our treatment of Christ, who suffered for us as an innocent lamb, scourged, and killed.

For many months, Gary mourned BSOB's death and would think he heard BSOB chirping, and tears would fall. Oh, how he missed him! BSOB had been with us for over fourteen years. We thought often about what he died of but came to wonder if he could have had heartworms. None of the vets that cared for BSOB mentioned that possibility, but it is known now that house cats can get them also.

BSOB taught me a lot about trust. He gave himself so totally to us, as his master. He overcame many of his animal instincts to become part of our life. Pondering BSOB's changes made me see my strong drive to remain stuck in sin. If we can give ourselves in trust to our God the way BSOB did, we become part of his family, a position that compares with none other. In the wild, BSOB would have lived probably not more than six years, if that. He enjoyed special privileges with us that he wouldn't have known. He never worried about food, hunters, the disappearing Florida glades he came from, or the small cage he had been condemned to. Likewise, God provides for us. The privileges we receive in the family of God are boundless. His promise is to be with us always, see us through all trials, and give us *life eternal*. I rejoice and thank Jesus daily.

While adjusting to the loss of BSOB, stories were retold of him again and again. One time in our house in the woods, three virile-looking young men came to visit—really to see BSOB. They had heard how much fun it was to play with him. Well, two of them went right out on the deck, but one just couldn't bring himself to make that move.

The other two played and wrestled with BSOB. Finally, laughing loudly, they burst into the bedroom where Gary was confined, healing another pressure sore. The one young gentleman that was left said in a quietly determined voice, "I'm going out there."

I thought he was the brave one, wrapped in fear, but still Wanting to do it.

BSOB would know it too!

I said, "Okay, but I will go with you."

We went out on the deck together. BSOB jumped up from below, walked slowly in his swaggering way past the stiff, not moving form of the young man. As he passed, he just picked up his paw and made a short swipe at the gentleman's pant leg. He moved on, but as

I watched in horror, the poor young man's pants became wet with the spot growing to cover his right pant leg.

Not knowing what to say, I tried to pull my eyes away. The young man mumbled, "Oh, I think BSOB has wet feet."

I thought to myself, "Well, he may have now."

We hurried inside, and he went the other way outside to the car to wait on the others. Holding it together until I heard the car leave, I then fell on the floor completely hysterical, laughing until I could not breathe.

From the bedroom, Gary yelled, "What's going on out there?"

Gasping, I went in to relate the story, and we had a riotous laugh at that poor young man's expense. But we knew he was the bravest of the three.

We laughed again remembering. I looked at my husband. He was brave too. I so wanted him to give his life to God. I wanted him to ask Jesus into his heart.

I prayed.

Slowly, we settled in, and Gary began working toward some of his goals. It was a big disappointment when plans fell through for him. If only people could have seen past the wheelchair and tap the talents he had.

Gary was not a quitter. We sold some trees for the finances to put up a workshop. Gary tried his hand at wood sculpture again. He began to make a swan planter, but out of his wonderful imagination came a beautiful swan wagon.

"This is for Josephine's first birthday," he said.

Her father took her for a ride in it, and before you could say Saskatchewan, Gary was busy carving swan wagons, which kept me busy sanding and painting. In fact, we got so busy that we needed help in cutting down and planing the lumber.

Gary got wind of an Amish man that might be of help. So into the van he piled, and with a wave, he was off to try to find him.

Finally finding the right farm, he drove in and honked.

Out rushed a firm-faced Amish woman. "Are you a salesman?" she inquired abruptly with a suspicious look in her eyes.

"No, not really," Gary said. "I'm in a wheelchair and cannot walk, so I didn't get out. I'm looking for some help in my little shop and wanted to talk to your husband about it."

"He's out in the field," she said, and she pointed Gary in the direction he might find him.

"Thank you," Gary replied, and he took off to meet Ora Mast.

Ora came to work for us, and that began a delightful learning time—a new friendship would permeate our life.

Every day, we made the trip to pick up Orie, as we now called him, and we began our day. Of course, Orie's day had started much earlier, as he was a dairy farmer. Cows needed to be milked in the morning and after we took him home at night. Orie was a blessing, and I was quite relieved to have someone else on the saws. Once I caught Gary pushing a large piece of wood through the saw by using his elbow to hit the joystick of his electric wheelchair. As the chair moved forward, the piece of wood moved through the saw. His fingers and face were so close to the blade, I cringed.

One weekend, Gary was working on the band saw and a piece of wood he was shaping flipped out of his hands. He cut both thumbs deeply, and I rushed him to the emergency room. Being the weekend, there were many little children ahead of us, so he was wrapped enough to help stop the flow of blood, and sat with his two thumbs elevated and straight up.

Of course, everyone asked, "What did you do?"

Gary grinned and said, "I fix pencil sharpeners!"

Some things never change!

Orie's happy disposition and sense of humor fit in very well with Gary and me. It was a joy to hear him whistle or sing while he worked. Many days I brought Tom out in the shop with us; he loved the sound of all the tools and hated to be alone. Tom liked to hear Orie whistle and followed right along, singing and whistling with him. I did warn Orie not to put his finger in Tom's cage because Tom was fearful of men with beards. Gary and I were out of the shop for a few minutes. Tom and Orie had been whistling together, and when I came back, Orie was standing looking at his bloody finger.

"I told you not to put your finger in that cage!"

"I know. I just thought I could pet him. He was whistling so nice with me. I know, I know, you told me!" He laughed.

We sent the graceful Swan Wagons to Canada, to Florida, to California, all over the country. Gary designed a Swan Sleigh, and they began to be popular also. As time went on, we tried taking sleighs and wagons to juried shows. That was a success too. It was a big undertaking to get Gary there with all the large wagons and sleighs. Both of us were so exhausted, trying to get them finished, we must have looked like we had pasted on smiles for the show.

Watching all the mothers come by and sigh sadly because they couldn't afford one of the wagons really hurt Gary. He knew we were not asking enough as it was for the time and money involved, and we were going to have to raise the price.

"I wish I could just make these and *give* them away," Gary said quietly, as he watched the young children reach for the swans.

My heart broke for him. He seemed especially tired lately, and to be truthful, I was more than a little tired myself.

Gary began doing small sculptures again, and I brought him a sketch of a Christmas card I had done many years before.

"This basic idea would make a beautiful nativity set, don't you think?"

Gary agreed, and he began work on it in cherry wood. With Gary's style and feel for the wood, wonderful things always happened. Mary, Joseph, and baby Jesus were all in a single piece, and there was one shepherd and one king. He worked on them many hours. They were about nine inches high and stunning. They were entered in the juried art show in Nappanee and won Best of Show, along with the purchase award. We needed the money for our van, but it broke my heart. I loved them so much, and still regret giving them up.

Orie's good nature and laughter did a lot to keep Gary going. There was a little spider that came every day to Gary's workbench. It actually sat there and watched him work.

"Don't you kill that spider," he told Orie. "He is my friend."

Orie would often stamp his foot and say, "*Oops*, I think I got your spider."

He would then laugh as Gary feigned anger before he broke into laughter too.

These were special days, but there were also sad spaces of time when we shed tears. We could never make one of these beautiful wagons for a grandchild. I longed and ached to see Laurie. Sometimes, I dreamed she suddenly walked through the door, laughing and radiating her crazy brand of fun.

Much pain was brought back to us when we lost Hooligan. He had made it back to Indiana but died at a friend's farm. I hated the fact that we didn't have him with us.

One day, I was invited to a luncheon with old school friends. As it always happens, after the "Do you remember?" was over, the conversation bounced to family, children, and grandchildren. Pain gripped me, and it was hard to concentrate. I turned to Jesus, praying for him to hold me up, enfold me in his love, and help me face the world with a joyful and thankful heart. He, of course, did!

I love the paraphrase in the Living Bible.

All your waves and billows have gone over me, and floods of sorrow pour upon me like a thundering cataract. Yet day by day, the Lord also pours out his steadfast love upon me, and through the night I sing his songs and pray to God who gives me life.

(Psalms 42:7–8, Living Bible)

Gary's endurance was on a dive downward, and I thought he should go to the doctor.

"I think there is too much redness around the opening where the Foley catheter goes into your bladder," I remarked. "There also seems to be more discharge in that area."

"Okay, let's get it looked at."

The doctor visit was unfruitful; he thought it was nothing. So we tried to be extra careful in cleaning around it and went on. No improvement came. In fact, it looked worse as the days went by.

We then went to see the urologist. After many tests and a trip to Indianapolis, the unexpected diagnosis hit us hard.

"You have cancer, Mr. Weatherwax," the doctor stated calmly. "Cancer of the bladder. It has progressed to the extent that the whole bladder must come out. We can try to build you a new bladder. That is really the only hope I can give you. Cancer treatments will not be of any help."

I looked at Gary's expression. Could he fight another battle? Could *we* fight another battle?

"We will talk it over," Gary said. The next few days were full of thick silences rather than frantic talk. When conversation erupted, it was short with well thought out words. It seemed as if an erratic wind was blowing around us, picking up speed and promising unknown crossings and trials.

We decided to go with the doctor's advice. A very long and difficult operation was performed in Indianapolis. I drove back and forth, trying to keep working in the shop to get some wagons out and money coming in. The aftermath of the operation was a nightmare. Gary was in terrible pain, taking strong medication, hallucinating continually, and of course, didn't want me to leave.

One of the nurses was quite abrupt, chiding me for not being there all the time. Then she made the remark that when they opened Gary up, he was full of cancer! I was shocked as that is not what I had been told. I thought she couldn't be right; they would have told me.

Finally coming home, we knew the recovery was going to be slow. But he didn't do as well as I expected. In a few months, he was very ill again, so we went back for more tests.

The trip home from Indianapolis was made in silence, as we both fought with the doctor's words, "You have two months to live."

Getting home, I helped him undress and get comfortable in bed. I sat beside him in the quiet and cried. We could talk tomorrow.

Father God,
Help us tonight.
Help us through the coming storm.
Father, I pray for Gary.
I pray he will give his life to you.
I love you.

CHAPTER 14

A new wind blows
to bite and sting our face.
We lean and push against it,
sick with its bitter taste.
Change this wind, God;
please hear my pleading cry;
Send this wind away to blow
in some far off empty sky.
Just help us now;
we're falling hard and fast.
All hope and strength are gone;
turn him to You God, at last.

We talked. We watched the squirrels playing in the trees and the birds at the feeder. We fed them in the summer as we both delighted in their beauty.

Gary began to worry about what I would do when he was gone. He wondered if I should keep trying to create Swan Wagons with Ora's help.

"Please do not worry about all that," I told him one day. "God will take care of me, I know."

It was almost twenty years since the accident that left Gary a paraplegic. His goal now was to make it until September third, which would be our thirty-fifth wedding anniversary.

I kept my early morning time with the ladies' prayer group. Leona Brandeberry asked, "Would you like to have an anointing and prayer for Gary's healing?

"Yes, but I will ask Gary first."

Gary consented. So one afternoon, there arrived at our home a pastor, Leona and her husband John, Laura Miller, and Barbara, Gary's sister.

We formed a circle beside Gary's bed and holding hands we prayed. The pastor anointed Gary with oil. My friend Tanya was on her way to California, but she was praying for Gary with others in the car at this exact same time.

> Is any sick among you? Let him call for the elders of the church; and let them pray over him, anointing him with oil in the name of the Lord: and the prayer of faith shall save the sick, and the Lord shall raise him up, and if he has committed sins, they shall be forgiven him.
>
> (James 5:14–15, KJV)

As we prayed, Gary's body seemed to light up, as if illuminated from the inside. There were tears streaming down everyone's faces, and we felt the presence of the Lord.

John said as they quietly left, "I do believe God has healed Gary."

We did not want to break the quiet peace we felt in the room, but after Barbara left, I began preparations for a meal.

Gary called me softly to his side. Looking at me with clear new eyes, he said, "Tell those wonderful people I am not physically healed, but I am spiritually healed!"

He truly was! Forgiven, born again, a changed child of God. He had fulfilled the divine design God had for him. Now he hungered for the word. I will forever remember Barbara coming for a visit and sitting beside Gary with her Bible, reading the sweet healing words of God's promise that Jesus spoke to Nicodemus, and to us all.

> For God so loved the world, that He gave His only begotten Son, that whosoever believeth in Him should not perish, but have everlasting life.
>
> (John 3:16, KJV)

The harsh wind was quieted and banished from Gary forever. He waited in peace for his moving day. A wonderful doctor visited him at home, and we tried to keep him as comfortable as possible.

One sunny day, while watching the birds through the little window at the end of the bed, I grinned and said, "When you are on the other side, and everything is A-okay, do you suppose you could ask God to send a scarlet tanager to the feeder?"

"I will," he said, smiling.

Before we went to Arizona, there were tanagers in the woods where we lived; we could see their breathtaking flashes from our front windows. They live in the deep woods so we did not see them on our open hill, and they are not known to come often to back yard feeders.

Gary had much pain and was drifting in and out of consciousness. Barbara came, and we knew this would be the last visit before his going home. My niece, Tina, visited in the evening hours. She told me later, she looked up to the night sky as she left, full of twinkling stars, and prayed God would release Gary. He did, and Gary went home.

He almost made it to September third. We would have been married thirty-five years.

Stepping from the shower, I wiped the steam from the mirror. The pale face staring from the fogged edges belonged to a stranger. So immersed in my husband's earth life ending, I had not seen myself for many months. The image does not please me, but I smiled. It did not matter.

Now I faced another change in my life. Alone, the word sounded strange. Alone, can I handle alone? For years, I only snatched minutes to be alone. Now the big empty space of alone seemed a little fearful. Going into the workshop, it was almost unbearable to let my eyes travel over to his carving bench. As I touched his tools, I felt heartbreak that his determined spirit would not be there creating beauty anymore. But I knew his ecstasy now was beyond my comprehension.

I turned and ran back to the trailer, calling Pia, his fragile little black cat. She had given Gary so much comfort in the last days of his life. Pia was always Gary's cat. After finding her under an abandoned trailer in Arizona, she spent most of her life on Gary's bed. Now she was lost and spent her time in the very back of the closet, refusing to eat. I truly thought she might die. I kept coaxing her to come out, then holding her, and tried to comfort her.

I smiled at the new pup at my feet. Blackie and Gal were both gone now, and when Gary knew he was dying, he thought I should get another German shepherd.

"I would rather wait," I had suggested gently. "The right one will come along."

"No, I think you should get it now," he answered determinedly.

I let the conversation end, but later in the evening, we began again.

"I saw an ad in the paper. They have purebred German shepherd puppies. Let's go look at them," Gary spoke with enthusiasm.

"I would rather not. It's a lot of work to start again with a puppy. I do not think I can handle it right now."

"It won't hurt to just take a look," Gary insisted.

Soon, we were on the road to look at German shepherd puppies. We found what we thought was the right place, and I knocked on the door. From around the corner of the house came a flood of pups.

This was the place. So Gary lowered the ramp and got out of the van. All the pups came wriggling and jumping, licking our hands, not a bit afraid of the wheelchair. All but one! She hung back, not looking fearful, but looking very cautious. She eventually warmed up, and Gary said that she was the one we should take.

"Just a minute," I whispered. "This whole litter does not look healthy." By that time, the lady of the house and the lady of the litter had arrived.

"They will be fine," he whispered back.

I shrugged my shoulders, sighed, and gave up.

"We'll take that little gal there," Gary told at the lady of the house. "That little pup stops and thinks things over. She's just what my wife needs! She will have a good home!"

We named the pup Sugar, and she *was* a good dog. Sugar also had a lot of health issues her whole life. Sugar was a wonderful companion in the hard days of change.

Pia finally decided I was the only game in town and started to eat again. Life goes on.

Orie and I tried to go on. The Swan Wagons were a work of art. There were hours of effort in each one. I would have to double the price, and I was getting into debt more each day. What do you want me to do, Lord? Help me!

Autumn tugged at my numbed senses, gently singing, and finally enveloping me in its shimmering spell. The pull to be in the midst of the color and crisp beauty won out many days. The heavy, old trees seemed to welcome my memories of tears and laughter. I sat with my back against their ridged bark, feeling every crook and gnarl. It was as if they shared every scar on my heart. Their soon-to-be bare branches moved in a comforting rhythm.

Then the rains came, soaking the leaf-covered ground and soaking my soul. Earth felt like a sponge as I slowly picked my way back and forth to fill the busy bird feeder. Sugar loved water in any form, so she happily accompanied me on these excursions. Shaking off the water, we burst into the house, and I ran to the window to watch the birds return. I rejoiced in the Blue Jays and Cardinals who made colorful dabs in the outdoor pallet of gray.

The soft sound of rain gave way to lightly spitting snow, and the coffee brewing filled the room with its inviting aroma. I was drawn to Gary's wheelchair in the corner. Touching it, I felt half of me was still in the worn leather back and cold steel frame. My husband and I were tied to a wheelchair for twenty years through pain, growing and joy. One half of me is empty. God, fill me.

The snow finally came. It was beautiful as large luminous flakes fell from a pure white sky. Sugar jumped, barked, and pried the kid out of me, so we played in our made over world.

Trying to go through the expected motions of Christmas, I ached just to spend the holidays quietly dreaming of other celebrations. Holidays filled with the shared love of Gary and my daughter, Laurie. They were both gone from my touch, but living vibrantly within me.

Winter seemed long, and the birds were telling their friends about my feeder. I counted thirteen Cardinals, accompanied by their shy ladies, all feeding at the same time. The pushy Jays and Woodpeckers sent the female Cardinals to the surrounding bushes. But the gallant mates grabbed a sunflower seed, flew to their lady fair, and gently presented it to her. Cardinals mate for life, as I think more humans would if we used the same gentle considerations.

Snow had lost its attraction, and I felt weary.

Chick-a-dee-dee, chick-a-dee-dee, the little black capped bird calls. "I'm so happy!" he sings, and I thought, *All well and good for you!*

His irresistible song finally charmed me into a better mood, and I smiled at his bright chatter. The sun was shining, and it was hard to look at the brightness bouncing off the snow.

A tiny stirring of hope for the spring began to grow in my heart. Walking to the feeder, I sensed it in the air, so did Sugar as she sniffed like it just might be coming today. Then she bounded off, burying her nose in the snow, making an interesting trail. I grinned as the cats intently watched from the window, understanding her fun.

Each day, I realized more and more I was not alone. Jesus was there with me every step of the way. I began to write love letters to Jesus; it seemed the most natural thing to do.

I received a phone call that sent me on a walk, and I returned to pen another letter.

Dear Jesus,

My friend is hurting. I feel deeply for her hurt, confusion, and rage. After her phone call, I searched for calm in a long walk. It is a gray, cold, and damp February day, yet my dog seemed unaware of the weather. She was overjoyed that we were going and showed interest in every little rock and shrub. She always stays close with that confident I'll-take-care-of-you look. I thank you for her, Jesus.

As we crested a hill, there was suddenly so much noise above that we both jumped and looked skyward. Above us was a beautiful red-tailed hawk flying strong and purposefully in a straight line. A large flock of screaming crows were taking turns diving at him, jabbing at him, and trying to throw him off course.

The hawk flew strong and calm, not losing a beat or dropping in altitude. This continued across the field. Eventually, the crows gave up and veered in another direction, cawing loudly. I watched as the hawk began to pick up the wind currents and soar in that wonderful way only hawks and eagles do.

Jesus, how great it is when we can be like that hawk, when all the darts of evil, temptation, despair, and trial are thrown at us, we keep on—straight and steady in your love and strength. When we have made it through, the sailing is so free and beautiful. I pray for my friend. I pray that she will turn to you, so you can hold her up and give her joy!

I love you.

But they that wait on the Lord shall renew their strength. They shall mount up with wings as eagles. They shall run and not be weary, they shall walk and not faint.

(Isaiah 40:31, KJV)

I was making some other items under Hushwing, the name of our business, and I decided to try my luck at a gift show in Chicago. My dear friend Maryellen, who was always ready for an adventure, came along to help. The show was a dismal failure. It cost me too much to attend, and my items attracted attention but were too expensive for most buyers.

Dear Jesus,

I took my wares to the gift show in the city. One has to look hard to find spirit-filled lives there. I prayed and vowed to keep you in my heart. It is easy to draw away from you and your word when in the market place. As we go about our earthly business, we are caught up in the competitive crunch and begin working with all our earthly senses and motives. Soon, we are feeling empty.

A beautiful, small, dark oriental woman came to my booth and looked at the display. She turned to me and said, "You must be a Christian!"

I smiled and in a small voice replied, "Ah well…Yes."

Oh dear Jesus, why didn't I shout it? Why didn't I share what you have done for me? Even by saying nothing, we can deny you. Forgive me.

I love you.

If anyone is ashamed of me and my words in this adulterous and sinful generation, the Son of Man will be ashamed of him when he comes in the Father's glory with the holy angels.

(Mark 8:38, NIV)

There were just patches of snow left and bright green shoots were confidently popping out. I felt like popping out too but not sure in what direction.

"Just follow the shoots and look upward," a curious, laughing little voice whispered.

With new vigor and a blazing hope, I was off again. "God, I trust you to lead and provide!"

It was easier to smile and dream, and suddenly some old, but not forgotten, creative juices were dancing in tune with the flowing early spring run off. A walk in the woods brought the tinkling sound of frozen water melting, a life giving music. Sugar was standing in the icy cold water with excitement in her eyes, and I seemed to catch some of it. We saw a robin.

Dear Jesus,

Last night was so beautiful. I was drawn outside. I climbed on the top of the picnic table and lay down just to gaze at the stars. My thoughts drifted back to when I was a little girl, always dreaming and wishing I could grow up and live in a forest. I felt such a longing for nature. There was a wonder and a beautiful ache I could not explain, like completeness just out of reach.

Oh dear Jesus, I felt it again last night. And suddenly, it became sparkling clear. Nature, created from God's beautiful perfect thoughts sparks a longing in me, but it really is a longing and desire for my Father in heaven.

Jesus, thank you for your time on earth, for showing us the path and giving us loving instructions on finding our Father.

I love you.

Oh Lord, our God, the majesty and glory of your name fills all the earth and overflows the heavens.

(Psalms 8:1, Living Bible)

It was soon apparent that I needed to do other work, or I was not going to make it. It was a sad day when we decided the Swan Wagons were not profitable enough to keep going, and Orie left.

Friends helped me constantly in these days of searching. I felt the stirring of a laughing wind. It beckoned me to open my eyes and heart to the gifts God had given me, and toss aside excuses of age, inexperience, fear of failure, and lack of resources. I had *lots* of sometimes funny, sometimes foolish failures. One was trying to open a gift shop in the room we had added to our trailer…talk about lack of ambiance. I started a string of various jobs: the school lunch room, cleaning, and the Salvation Army, which was a complete disaster. In slang terms, you might say, "I gave away the store," but to copy a Gary trait, I kept on keeping on!

I do believe when you have totally sold out to Jesus and have been born again, the Holy Spirit that lives within you does not look the other way when you sin. You are brought up short, knowing your words were not true, or they were hurtful to another. So it was with me.

Dear Jesus,

My heart is burdened today. Once again, I have spoken words better left unsaid. What damage

I have done, I do not know. Why is it so difficult to control my mouth?

From this day forward, I will think of my words as flowers. Beautiful flower words that put joy in hearts, celebrate life, give love, and show sympathy, tenderness and concern. Flowers that give the wonderful radiance of your word and the fragrance of the Holy Spirit.

I love you.

Let the words of my mouth, and the meditation of my heart, be acceptable in thy sight, O Lord, my strength and my redeemer.

(Psalms 19:14, KJV)

These days were full of learning to trust the Lord. He would provide at the very last minute, whatever the need. This was a time of humbling, the awareness that it wasn't through *my* talents or *my* strength that my problems were solved. It was through *his* grace, *his* strength, and *his* love. Over and over with nowhere to turn, he opened a door.

The summer months had gone by quickly. When I was small, it seemed they went on forever. Now the days fluttered past like a beautiful butterfly drifting from one flower to another.

The warm days were hanging on, and I was having morning devotions at my little table with the windows open. I glanced out towards the bird feeder. I couldn't believe what I was seeing! There was this bright scarlet bird with black wings! It did not feed, just looked at me for an instant and was gone. A scarlet tanager, it *had* to be a scarlet tanager! I couldn't move. I just sat there and cried tears of joy. I began to come to Jesus without a request, just the desire to be with him…just be with him.

> Dear Jesus,
>
> Today, I just want to spend some time with you. I do not want to ask for anything or pray for anyone. I do not need to hear your voice, but just want to be quiet in your presence. I want to tell you how beautiful your colors are, how gentle your smile, how wonderful your love, and how much I adore you.
>
> Your radiance fills my heart and soul and gives me peace. I am your servant.
>
> Jesus, I love you.
>
> Be still, and know that I am God. I will be exalted among the nations. I will be exalted in the earth!
>
> (Psalms 46:10, NIV)

I prayed for guidance in choosing a church. God led me to First Baptist.

I prayed for the right job. God led me to a school as a special education aide.

I prayed for God to shape me into a sharp, clean tool he can use. He's working on it!

I think of the radiance of God and how it filled Gary, shining for all of us to see. I think of my cousin, Nina, an amazingly strong lady, who was confined to a wheelchair from a little girl until her death. Her life was a textbook on human determination. Nina crawled out of her chair to plant and care for a garden. She ran a gift shop in her home. She cooked, cleaned, and took care of her invalid, bedridden Mother from a wheelchair. This meant bedpans and changing sheets continually. Nina spurned help, even from God. A lady came to her house to talk to her about Jesus, and Nina told her to leave. Nina was finally in the hospital dying, without any strength or control over what was happening to her. I visited her, grieved by her contorted face and the apparent anguish she was experiencing.

I took her hand and talked to her about Jesus. When I was through, she managed to whisper, "I believe."

She relaxed, and I left the room for a few minutes. When I returned, I saw the radiance of God in Nina's face. She was quiet, not struggling as before, and there was peace. She shared with me something that she wanted to make right. She met her Maker that night.

My sister Jean lost her husband to cancer, and months later, she was dying from cancer too. I made the trip to Danville as often as I could to be with Jean. Many times, my dear friend Tanya came with me, and she prayed and loved my sister right along with me. We watched in awe. As Jean came closer and closer to death, she became more radiant, right though her suffering.

One day, I whispered to my sister, "I wish I could take your pain for you."

Her reply was, "Oh, this is nothing compared to what my Jesus suffered for me."

Tanya watched with me in wonder as Jean came closer and closer to Jesus, and the light in her face shone so beautifully. That last trip home before she was gone, Tanya and I sang joyful hymns all the way back. That's a lot of singing from near Indianapolis to Elkhart. Our car seemed to lift and ride above the road on air. Tanya looked at me in amazement. She said, "This car feels like it is floating above the ground." As we sped around Elkhart in the dark, on the bypass headed for Middlebury, we both glanced out the window to the left at the same time. A huge ball of light with a fiery tail burned across the sky, gone as fast as it came. We were stunned, and yet somehow exhilarated.

The next day, we tried to find out if anyone else had seen it. No one had. It was not reported anywhere. We still do not know anything about it, except that we took it as our sign: God was with us.

I pray all who read these words will come to know our Lord and Savior. I pray the brilliant and resplendent light of Jesus will shine from you on this darkened world.

Keep your feet grounded in the word, but raise your hands up to catch the glorious and glittering dusting from heaven on your life. A life serving Jesus is no boring existence: it is an exciting adventure!

The end of this story is really the beginning. The day was bright, but soft. The sunshine showered on everything, but a light, dancing breeze tickled the tall grass to flutter and rustle.

I sat on the back porch of my beautiful cabin that was a gift from God through my gracious and fabulously generous niece, Heidi. This divinely wonderful day seemed to say…write. I picked up a pen, the clean, white paper before me, and began to write the words the Lord gave me.

It fans the fire in my heart,
softly laughs across my skin.
Listening to your gentle song
I'm dancing in the wind.

Winds shift, blow hard and strong
to push me into sin;
I turn my face toward your flame,
I'm dancing in the wind.

Dear God, I feel your covering wings
lift me from within;
Your rhythm deep lives in my soul,
I'm dancing in the wind.